Advance Praise

"Stress and anxiety are not your enemy. They are simply a part of life for all humans, especially high-functioning individuals. Making big decisions, facing adversity, and being your best self requires confronting and dealing with these emotions! FINALLY, the narrative on stress and anxiety is changing, thanks to Dr. Rebecca Heiss. *Springboard* is a must-read for all!"

—**David H. Rosmarin,** Associate Professor at Harvard Medical School, Founder of Center for Anxiety, and Author of *Thriving with Anxiety: 9 Tools to Make Your Anxiety Work for You*

"In an era of endless self-help noise, this book stands apart through its rare combination of scientific rigor and charming narrative, helping its readers recognize the power they have in shifting stress to truly serve them. Your future self will thank you for reading this."

—**Rachel DeAlto,** Communication and Relatability Expert and Author of *Relatable: How to Connect with Anyone Anywhere (Even if It Scares You)* and *The Relatable Leader*

"Stop managing stress—start mastering it. Dr. Heiss shows you how to turn fear into fuel and leap forward into your one wild, precious life."

—**Dan Waldschmidt,** Ultra-runner, Reader, and CEO at Panzura

"STRESS! Just hearing the word USED TO give us anxiety . . . but Dr. Rebecca Heiss's new book *Springboard* has offered us a completely new way to think about this power source. Rebecca's reinterpretation of stress affords us the opportunity to actually USE stress to our benefit. With her sense of humor, contagious energy, and relatable stories, Rebecca explores how anxiety can be reframed as a catalyst for motivation, creativity, and personal growth. We read many books for our podcast, and *Springboard* really stands out by offering tools to channel this 'tiger' in a way that not only helps you overcome obstacles but also propels you forward toward success. It's an empowering read for anyone looking to turn stress into a source of strength, focus, and momentum."

—Jean Trebek and Alison Martin, Co-hosts of the
insidewink podcast

"Rebecca Heiss's *Springboard* is a revelation! A transformative guide and game changer for anyone looking to harness stress as a catalyst for growth and innovation. Her novel approach isn't about managing stress—it's about mastering it to fuel performance, creativity, and joy. *Springboard* is a must-read for leaders and individuals aiming to thrive in today's fast-paced world."

—Josh Linkner, 5x Tech Entrepreneur, *New York Times* Bestselling Author, Venture Capital Investor, and Professional Jazz Guitarist

SPRINGBOARD

SPRING BOARD

Transform STRESS to work for you

DR. REBECCA HEISS

IDEAPRESS
PUBLISHING

WASHINGTON, DC

IDEAPRESS
PUBLISHING

Ideapress Publishing | www.ideapresspublishing.com

All trademarks are the property of their respective companies.

Cover Design: Kendra Cagle, 5 Lakes Design

Interior Design: Kendra Cagle, 5 Lakes Design

Author photo: Brian Knox

Editorial Director: Kameron Bryant-Sergejev

Copy Editor: Christina Caruccio

Cataloging-in-Publication Data is on file with the Library of Congress.

Hardcover ISBN: 978-1-64687-199-5
eBook: 978-1-64687-211-4
Audiobook: 978-1-64687-212-1

Special Sales

Ideapress books are available at a special discount for bulk purchases for sales promotions and premiums or for use in corporate training programs. Special editions, including personalized covers, a custom foreword, corporate imprints, and bonus content, are also available.

1 2 3 4 5 6 7 8 9 10

Dedication

For my pack,
my tribe,
my warriors,
my GAMECHANGERS.

Table of Contents

PART I

LOADING THE SPRING

The day I blew up my entire life started just like any other. The panic had crept in slowly.

During my tenure as a teacher, I met a good man who fell in love with me, and whom I loved. So, I got married. I bought a home. And just like that, I had a life. I had everything I was supposed to want: a good partner who loved me, a stable job, a nice home. I had carefully constructed what *looked* like the perfect life.

And I was dying inside.

Not because anything was wrong. But because nothing was right.

Was this really what I was going to do until I died? Wake up, go teach, come home exhausted, walk the dogs, cook dinner, rinse, repeat. There was nothing out of place. Nothing overtly *wrong* with this life. Except it didn't feel like a life. It felt like a sentence I was serving. I kept waiting for my real life to start. I had carefully and successfully weeded out all of the big risks: I hadn't stretched too far for love, lest I set myself up for heartbreak. I hadn't overextended myself in my career, lest I be proven not up for the task. I had no tigers chasing me—no major stressors to fret about. I'd secured my future. I'd mastered the game. So why wasn't I feeling fulfilled? Why wasn't I finding meaning and purpose in my life?

What if the stress we are all trying to avoid is the very thing that gives our lives meaning, excitement, and purpose?

A phone call from my sister set my whole life spinning like a top. Her voice cracked as she told me that her wife of twenty years, a second sister to me, had an inoperable brain tumor. At best, she had a year to live. My heart slammed against my ribcage, every beat echoing the poet Mary Oliver's famous line . . .

"Doesn't everything die at last, and too soon?
Tell me, what is it you plan to do with your
one wild and precious life?"

One wild and precious life.

One wild and precious life.

In the wake of the sobering mortality I felt hanging up the phone, I began reviewing my own life, recognizing that had that been *my* diagnosis, I'd be devastatingly disappointed with the life I'd led. I made every decision up to that point out of fear, playing it safe. I'd avoided the riskier career I'd wanted to pursue. I'd settled for a stable relationship over passionate love. I'd chosen to live in comfort rather than in a place that made my heart race.

That month, I did what most people would call crazy. I quit my job. I sold my house. I divorced my husband. For the first time, I began to bet on myself. On my research. On the fact that our stress isn't something to be avoided, but embraced as our cocreator in building a wild and precious life. Was I terrified? Absolutely. But here's what I've learned: Terror is fuel if you know how to use it. It was time to start truly living . . . which meant taking my own medicine when it came to inviting stress to the table. The journey was, of course, uniquely my own. But I realized that as I stepped into my life with stress as my cocreator, more people opened up to me about their dreams, stressors, failures, and hopes, and I discovered that my story is your story, and your story is mine. This book isn't about my journey. It's about yours. So many of us are waiting to live. We're teetering on the edge of fear and unwilling to answer the door when we know that stress waits on the other side. My hope for you is that you will fling open the door and invite our friend stress in for tea. Meaning, purpose, and joy will greet you on the other side of the doorway, and you'll not get there without stress. One wild and precious life awaits—yours.

Chapter 1

Changing the Narrative on Stress

Objective:
Begin to question why we label stress as "bad."

When did you first learn that stress was bad? I don't mean to blame and shame any of us who believe this story, but I do think that stress needs a better PR agent. Why do we believe stress is bad for us? My guess is that most of us would quickly reference the hundreds of news articles that are published each day, many of which contain some version of the headline: "Stress is killing you!" Fair enough. But the same would have to be said of oxygen.

Seriously.

Can you imagine a headline that read: "Oxygen is killing you!"? But the science would be just as valid. While oxygen is essential for human life, it is also inherently dangerous and often, ultimately, what kills many of us, rusting us slowly from the inside out over the course of our lifetimes. Oxygen is truly toxic. As it metabolizes in our bodies, oxygen spews off free radicals, which damage our bodies' proteins, lipids, and even our DNA, often leading to mutations and potential cancer.[1] The process of oxidation is the reason we age.

But you'll never hear anyone say we should get rid of oxygen or scroll across headlines that say: "Oxygen: the silent killer!"

Why? Because we understand that oxygen, despite its dangers, is essential for life.

I think our culture has consciously and unconsciously reshaped (through millions of interactions, teachings, and media stories) stress into a catchall for a range of challenges in our human condition. Part of my mission for this book is to redefine stress so it doesn't immediately make people pull back in horror at its mention. We're all stressed. It's the air we breathe. But just like oxygen, our aim shouldn't be to rid stress from our lives but to use it to our advantage.

I've spent decades dedicated to better understanding our relationship with stress and the paradoxes of its effects on us. For example, if you go for a run, you put your body under a tremendous amount of stress.[2] Your heart pounds, you sweat, you produce cortisol, and you elevate the amount of sugar in your bloodstream. But this is supposed to be healthy, right? It is. Stress your body with exercise and it's good. But have those same stress responses (elevated heart rate, sweat, cortisol, high blood sugar) while you're stuck in traffic on your way to work, and you're well on your way to a coronary event! Just like oxygen, stress gives our body life; and just like oxygen, it can take it away. This is the stress paradox that nobody's talking about.

The promise of this book is intended to help us understand how we can welcome stress into our lives the way we welcome the air we breathe. The less we fight against stress, the more powerfully we can use it to our advantage.

Let me be crystal clear about something: You, my reader, will not feel less stressed after reading this book.

If that's what your aim is, put the book down now. I can't help. But neither can anyone else in the wellness industry looking to take your money in exchange for a life where you experience less stress. Stressful events will continue to happen to us all.

What I can promise you, is that after reading this book, you will develop a new relationship with stress.

One where you recognize stress for what it is—energy to be molded and shaped for your own utility, and quite often the very catalyst for living a meaningful life. After all, Olympic athletes don't break world records at practice. They break them when the pressure and stress is at its highest. We can all perform at the highest level under pressure when we change our stress mindset.

I've had the honor of working with professional athletes, CEOs and teams of Fortune 500 companies, stay-at-home parents, college students, and now you. Thousands of people have benefited from transforming their stress mindset and using it as a springboard to unlock their greatest potential. When you're ready, make the jump, bet on yourself, and let's springboard forward in our stress together.

The first step?

Understanding why getting rid of stress is the wrong goal entirely...

Chapter 2

The Only People with Zero Stress Are Dead

Objectives:

1. Recognize that stress isn't going away.
2. Understand that trying to get rid of stress is a misguided goal.

Let me throw some familiar stats about stress at you.

We are currently witnessing an unprecedented rise in the symptoms of stress, anxiety, and depression. Year after year, the news on mental health only seems to worsen. Studies show that "normal" children today report more anxiety than child psychiatric patients did in the 1950s![3]

Let that sink in.

Our children are more anxious than kids who needed psychiatric help seventy years ago! This alarming trend is not confined to children alone. Adults, too, are experiencing a significant increase in mental-health disorders. In fact, during the first year of the COVID-19 pandemic, the global prevalence of anxiety and depression increased by a massive 25 percent.[4]

And here's what's crazy: We're trying harder than ever to fight stress and anxiety. The self-help trend has risen astronomically in popularity, with Google searches for "self-care" increasing 315 percent since 2017.[5] The global wellness industry also grew 12.8 percent from 2015 to 2017, from a $3.7 trillion market to a $4.2 trillion market.[6] The number of people meditating more than tripled between 2012 and 2017,[7] and according to a Harvard Health survey, the number of Americans doing yoga has grown by over 50 percent in four years.[8]

SO, THE BIG QUESTION IS, WITH ALL THIS ATTENTION ON SELF-HELP, WHY AREN'T WE GETTING BETTER?

We're spending billions on stress management techniques, but those alarm bells just keep getting louder!

Here's something even more shocking: A study recently published in *Industrial Relations Journal* explored the outcomes of ninety workplace wellness programs and interventions—apps, coaching, relaxation classes, courses in time management, etc.—and surprisingly found that these programs had **no positive**

effect.[9] In fact, the trainings around stress management seemed to have made matters worse!* Quite a damning study if you're in the field of stress management!

In a *New York Times* article from January 2024, Tony D. LaMontagne, a professor at Deakin University, pointed out that these programs might be making people feel like it's their fault if they're still stressed after participating.[10] This could lead people to think they're failing *(Maybe I'm a loser and there really is no hope for me!)*, when that's not the case.

This sentiment echoed a 2019 interview of Michael Ungar, a professor of social work and a family therapist who suggests that the self-help industry unintentionally promotes victim-blaming: "If it doesn't work out, then somehow the onus ends up on you, that you just didn't attend enough Oprah seminars, or sit long enough on your yoga mat, or do the mindfulness-based stress reduction practice, or you just didn't have enough grit to overcome the fact that you have a really, really toxic boss."[11]

Oof! What an awful (and opposite) feeling of the intended relief that stress management programs are meant to provide! What is going wrong with all of our well-intentioned efforts toward wellness?

We are working with a broken model. The wellness industry has been focused on the wrong things.

---

*There was one notable exception which *did* improve well-being: a stress intervention that encouraged workers to do charity or volunteer work. The reason for this exception will be examined more closely in chapters 7 and 8.

All the attention and effort has been put into the twofold idea that:

1. **Stress is killing us.**
2. **Therefore, we must reduce or eliminate stress.**

But stress isn't going anywhere, and often, that stress is far beyond our control. The idea that we'll ever be rid of it is a farce at best. The only people who have zero stress are dead people, and our aim should not be death! But having zero or very little stress in one's life seems to be the common goal. I hear refrains of this echoing all the time in our culture:

- *"I need to get rid of all my stress so I can actually focus!"*
- *"If only I could go to a desert island somewhere and sip mai tais, I would truly be content with my life."*
- *"I just need to run away and start over. Start fresh. Start with no stress!"*

This is the point in the conversation when I pull out a marker and draw an upside-down U to represent the Yerkes-Dodson curve—a description of how well we typically perform based on our levels of stress.

The curve you see here is the traditional model of the relationship between stress and task performance. The Yerkes-Dodson curve suggests that to reach your peak level of performance, you need to achieve an intermediate level of stress, or arousal. Too little arousal (you are lying around on a beach, for example) or too much arousal (probably whatever state you're in now that led you to pick up this book) results in poorer performance.[12]

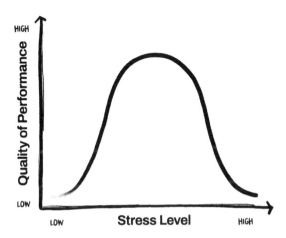

I think it's important to point out exactly how this model was devised. In the original experiment in 1908, Robert Yerkes and John Dodson used electric shocks to understand learning in mice. The mice received a mild shock when they entered a white box, but no shock if they entered an adjacent black box.

Initially, the researchers applied very weak shocks, which resulted in the mice taking a long time before consistently choosing the black box over the white one. As the shock intensity increased, the mice learned to avoid the white box more quickly. However, when the shocks were at their strongest, the learning rate slowed down again.

Over the years, the Yerkes-Dodson law has seen a variety of interpretations and extrapolations with frequent mentions in business application and work stress levels,[13] despite the fact that the original experiment was limited to only a small number of mice. The traditional focus of stress management has been on trying to reduce our stress—or, in some cases, to push us up the curve with more stress to enhance performance—walking this delicate balance beam between too little and too much in order to hit that sweet spot along the Yerkes-Dodson curve. You can likely already appreciate how difficult this is to measure for yourself, let alone for anyone you're trying to manage or coach. What is too much stress for one person will not be enough for another. How is anyone supposed to find that peak where performance is maximized, let alone maintain it consistently? I don't think you can. This model is precisely why these stress-management programs have been failing left and right.

I want to be clear: It's not that yoga or meditation is bad. Over two hundred studies find that mindfulness-based therapy can be effective for reducing stress, anxiety, and depression.[14] I'm a huge advocate for engaging in these practices (and shoot, just a night of binging Netflix on the couch and forgetting about everything for a while can be an incredible respite). But eventually, we have to reengage, and this is where the issues seem to emerge. A 2013 study found that as people tried to cope with stress through "release and avoid" practices, their goal of avoiding stress actually led to worse long-term outcomes like depression, divorce, and getting fired.[15]

Our relationship with stress needs to shift from avoiding and suppressing it to welcoming and engaging with it.

BECAUSE WE DON'T NEED CALM:
We need control in the chaos when our stress responses have been activated.

It's time to overhaul your relationship with stress, beginning with understanding why everything you've been taught about managing stress is likely working against you.

Chapter 3

The Emergence of a New Model

Objectives:

1. Stop labeling stress as good or bad.
2. Begin seeing stress as energy that can be deployed in our favor.

We deserve a better relationship with stress than what the wellness industry has been offering. Avoidance, after all, isn't just unhealthy—it's often just not possible.

Let me paint you a picture of what stress looks like for most of us:

You're trying to focus at work, but your phone won't stop pinging. Emails flood your inbox faster than you can clear them. Your calendar looks like a game of Tetris gone wrong.

At home, the laundry's piling up, dinner needs cooking, and your family needs attention. Oh, and you're supposed to find time for self-care somewhere in there too.

Sound familiar? This was the impetus for our 2024 research project, in which we explored the stress mindset of over 750 adults.

We wanted to better understand:

1. How stressed-out Americans were

2. How well current stress-reduction techniques were working

3. How a new approach to stress could help

What we found was staggering. At any given moment, most Americans rate their stress levels between 75 to 90 out of 100! That's like living in constant high alert.

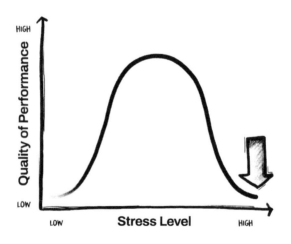

But the prescriptions for dealing with this often only succeeded in making stress worse. Maybe you take a break from the kids, escape the house, and do a bit of yoga, but when you return, you find your heart rate spikes right back up as you juggle all the shifting schedules and help the kids with their homework (When did sixth-grade math get that hard?!). Or, perhaps you take that vacation you've needed and get a bit of relief, but when you return to meetings, traffic, and your overflowing inbox, you're right back to where you started (or worse!), feeling devoid of hope that you'll ever be free of the stress. "Me time" too often means returning to work overtime!

The reality is that in a world with ever-increasing demands, this fear that you'll always be scrambling may be legitimate. Stress isn't going anywhere. We can push back on it all we want, but we are fighting a losing battle. Our research found that over 58 percent of Americans stress out even more when trying to control their stress! Let that sink in. We're making ourselves more stressed by trying not to be stressed! Not the most ideal outcome. We find ourselves in a clash against something like the ancient Greek hydra monster—a stress beast that resprouts double the number of heads we just chopped off. Or, perhaps doomed like Sisyphus, we feel forced to roll the boulder of our stress back to an almost manageable point, only to have it roll right back down the performance hill. But unlike those in the Greek mythological tales, we are not doomed to repeat this cycle for eternity.

OUR FOCUS NEEDS TO SHIFT.

Rather than trying to reduce or eliminate stress, we need to use stress to our advantage.

I suspect most of us have heard of the concept of *eustress* (or *"good stress"*) before. It's the kind of stress that helps us to function and motivates us. Think about how that approaching deadline gets you going on a totally manageable project. You can see how eustress leads us up the performance curve before reaching the point of overwhelm and *distress* (the kind of "bad stress" we usually are referencing with the word "stress") on the traditional outline of the Yerkes-Dodson curve.

But I want to offer a new model...

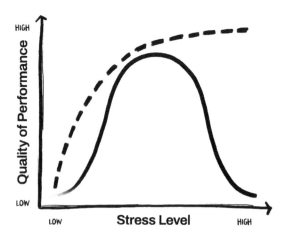

. . . a vision where there is no real good or bad stress in our lives. Rather than fight against it, we can use stress (in all its forms) to springboard us to our highest levels of performance, passion, and purpose. When framed properly, any stress can be used to move us toward our goals (whatever they might be) in a manner that offers more meaning and joy along the way. That's not to say that stress is always good. Certainly, the last thing I want to do is create some Pollyanna vision of stress, where I lead my readers to feel like they should be happy about the loss of a job or a difficult divorce or some other challenging situation we are all destined to encounter. The model I outline isn't meant to judge stress as good or bad. Rather, it's simply to acknowledge that stress is merely energy in our bodies, and we have the power to convert it in a manner that launches us toward the most productive, healthy direction available.

That's the theory (and practice) behind the **FEAR[less] Stress Formula.** It's a technique developed through years of research and thousands of hours of practice, both personally and with clients and teams.

Our research in 2024 focused on measuring the effectiveness of this formula in the form of a journaling exercise designed to mediate stress as measured by:

1. **The Perceived Stress Scale (PSS):** A validated stress assessment originally developed in 1983 to assess how feelings and thoughts contribute to stress over the course of the previous month.[16] Participants completed the PSS before the start of the trial and at the end of thirty days of practicing the FEAR[less] Stress Formula via a journaling activity.

2. **Heart Rate Variability (HRV):** A measure of time between heartbeats that is often used to assess stress levels and can be indicative of other psychological states like anxiety, fatigue, and burnout.[17] Higher HRV generally signifies a more adaptive response to stress.

The results were profound. After a thirty-day period:

- *85 percent of participants demonstrated a reduction in their Perceived Stress Scale*
- *40 percent of participants reported an increase in their HRV*

But the numbers themselves don't tell the whole story. Participants were eager to share other unsolicited insights, such as...

"I haven't had a resting heart rate that low for two years!"

and

"I'm finding that I have been having less anxiety, which is incredible, and some days I don't have fears to write about at all!"

Another participant wrote,

"Transformative: at my life stage this was an absolute perfect time to participate in this journey. The daily prompt to focus on my fears became an exercise in self-honesty that feels like an accelerator for my journey of contribution. I'm better for not just myself but for everyone around me for having participated in this technique."

It is my belief that anyone can achieve these results when we extend beyond the limited, often victim-blaming narrative of self-care to offer a broader framework for coping with and thriving in stress. Anyone can achieve these results. You don't need special equipment. You don't need hours of free time.

You just need to understand three simple steps:

1. Acknowledge it's not a tiger *(yes, really—I'll explain)*
2. Transfer the energy
3. Set your trajectory

In the next few chapters, I'm going to break down each of these steps in detail.

LET'S START WITH THE TIGERS...

Want a chance to participate in the research?[18]

 Start your <u>PRE-TRIAL</u> by taking the PSS assessment by scanning this QR code and then follow the original protocol below.

Record your pre-trial PSS score here: _____

If you have a fitness tracker, you can average your last thirty days of HRV and record it here: _____

For the next thirty days, you'll participate in a seven-minute journaling exercise based on my FEAR[less] Stress Formula. You can do your first journal entry here, but then I'd recommend using this exercise as an excuse to go out and buy yourself a nice new journal for the next twenty-nine entries. You can journal at any time of day, but my recommendation is just before you head to bed or when you first wake up in the morning. Science demonstrates that pairing a new habit (like journaling) with one you've already established (brushing your teeth) can help you stay consistent. Each day, journal using the three steps below.

Step 1

TIGER

This is where we move all of our fears from the emotional, irrational, limbic part of our brains onto the page. Set a timer for three minutes and simply spew out all the ways you fear your stressor will unfold. Let your imagination go wild, and write out the worst-case scenario.

Our brains need these three minutes of screaming terror!

That's what our stress response was built for. Don't try to suppress anything. You don't have to be rational during this phase. Give into the stress and go *through* it by putting it onto the page. When the timer goes off, ask yourself the question, *Is it a tiger?*

Will this stressor kill and eat you in the next three minutes? If not, the fight/flight/freeze response your body is experiencing can be reframed to help you.

_____

_____

_____

_____

_____

_____

_____

_____

_____

_____

_____

_____

_____

_____

Is it a tiger? ◯ YES ◯ NO

Step 2
TRANSFER

You've made it past the three minutes of screaming terror and have signaled to your brain that you've "outrun" the tiger. You're no longer in imminent danger. By writing down the fear and stress, you've activated your frontal lobe—the executive functioning part of your brain—and can now explore how this ordeal might become an adventure.

Curiosity and fear cannot coexist.

THERE IS NO BRAIN MECHANISM THAT ALLOWS US TO BE CURIOUS WHEN WE ARE ALSO FEARFUL.

Our human brains simply didn't evolve the capacity to ask questions when tigers were charging us (probably for the best!). But we can use this adaptation as a feature: By asking questions and developing a new narrative for our stress (i.e., "My body is preparing me to perform"), we create positive affirmations and stories that have been scientifically shown to significantly improve our health, deepen our relationships, and positively impact our business outcomes.

Spend the next two minutes writing about the following prompts:

- *What good could come of this?*
- *What adventure might I have?*
- *What story might help me succeed through the stress?*
- *What might I learn from this?*
- *How will I grow?*

_____

_____

_____

_____

_____

_____

_____

_____

_____

_____

_____

_____

Step 3
TRAJECTORY

By taking some small action forward you activate the "winners' cycle," increasing dopamine (a motivation hormone) and signaling to your body that you can use this stress to overcome big things by starting small. Recognizing that our stress energy can also benefit others is another key to helping us set a healthy trajectory.

Spend the next two minutes writing about the following prompts:

- *What is the smallest possible way to move forward?*

- *When you are through the stressful period, what meaning will you derive from it?*

- *What benefit does your stress have for helping those on your team, in your family, or in your community at large?*

_____

_____

_____

_____

_____

_____

_____

_____

_____

_____

_____

_____

_____

_____

_____

_____

_____

_____

_____

_____

_____

_____

_____

_____

_____

_____

_____

_____

_____

_____

_____

_____

 After you've completed the journaling exercise for thirty days, complete the POST-TRIAL PSS assessment and record your results here: _____

After you've completed the journaling exercise for thirty days, record your average HRV data here: _____

PART II

THE FEAR (less) STRESS FORMULA

In an article for *Greater Good* Berkeley, famed Stanford stress physiologist and bestselling author Robert Sapolsky quips that "for 99 percent of the species on this planet, stress is three minutes of screaming terror in the savannah, after which either it's over with or you're over with."[19]

Stage 1
THE TIGER

The **Tiger** stage of my FEAR[less] Stress Formula is a nod to Sapolsky, meant to represent these first three minutes of screaming terror. Perhaps you are running for your life away from an actual tiger, but more than likely, the "tiger" that's chasing you is a modern-day version. Tigers on the Savannah have morphed into a snarling inbox at your office or a scary meeting in which you must present to the board. In the case of contemporary humans, the tiger isn't typically something that is going to actually kill and eat us, but our biology isn't wise to that. This is why, in this stage, we will have the same physiological response to running late and hitting a traffic jam as we would to a dash for our lives away from a predator. Our challenge, then, in this first phase of the FEAR[less] Stress Formula, isn't to avoid the tiger; it's actually to lean into it. Go ahead and take the ride up that physiological state of arousal.

We want (even need!) stress in our lives to make them meaningful...

but first, we need to get clear that the stressor is
NOT A REAL TIGER.

Even if it feels that way in the moment, even if it is a tiger in waiting—a terminal diagnosis, for example, that will eventually kill and eat us—if we won't be dead in the next three minutes, we get to enjoy the ride up the physiological high of inviting our stressor in. Our hearts will pound, our mouths will dry up—but without a real tiger actively chasing us, we get to choose how we respond. We can move, run, fight, and take action. The tiger is an invitation to rise to a challenge we accept.

Stage 2
THE FEAR[less] TRANSFER

The **FEAR[less]** stage is where all the stress, anxiety, and fear energy is transferred from a state of worry and negative stress to a proactive state. We aren't fearless: We are fearing less. In other words, the heightened arousal state is still there, but we are beginning to transfer that energy toward an adventure. The FEAR[less] stage begins to lift off from the traditional downward arc of the Yerkes-Dodson curve by embracing the layers of stress as excitement, anger, or possibility. Removing the label of bad stress and leaning into it doesn't mean that you need to be happy about events that cause fear or sadness, only that you don't need to try to be (and quite frankly can't be!) calm in the fear. At heightened physiological states, it's easier to find another heightened arousal emotion that we can work with (i.e., excitement or anger) rather than trying to dissipate that energy to achieve some semblance of calm. We convert all the energy that stress provides into a usable form that carries us forward.

THIS BECOMES OUR SPRINGBOARD—
our competitive advantage.

Stage 3
THE SPRINGBOARD

As Lewis Carroll so aptly pointed out in *Alice in Wonderland*, "If you don't know where you are going, any road will get you there."[20] The **Springboard** stage, then, points your transferred stress energy down the road you wish to take. In other words, how will you use it? Setting a trajectory helps us to channel and focus our energy toward something we wish to achieve. This doesn't guarantee the outcome of any goal of course, but it begins to give us the data we need to continually adapt and adjust to the stress over time, moving in the direction that brings meaning to our lives and ensuring that we are in service to ourselves and those around us.

Whether you're looking for an edge in your career or are struggling with the overwhelm of daily stressors, this approach will offer you a new, deeper understanding and appreciation for embracing the stress in your life.

The decision to implement it is yours.

Chapter 4

Inviting the Tiger in for Tea

Objectives:

1. **Acknowledge the stress. Don't fight against it.**
2. **Lean into the stressor, realizing it is not a tiger** *(something that will kill and eat you in the next three minutes).*
3. **Go for a ride up the physiological activation levels and find comfort in recognizing that you aren't alone.**

Subway Tigers

Our brain is quite convinced that most things in life are tigers. For example, getting rejected or failing in front of your peers can feel just as painful as the sharp edges of a tiger's tooth.

Literally.

While sitting in the safety of our living rooms reading stories about rejection or failure, we know how ridiculous it would be to fear, for example, the rejection of a stranger, but the fear becomes palpable when we experience rejection ourselves. Famed Yale social psychologist Stanley Milgram once ran an experiment in which he asked his students to request that people on the New York subway give up their seats for them. After his students complained about how difficult the task was, even describing the experience as traumatic, this famous psychologist set out to do it himself in order to demonstrate to his students that they were being weak and complaining over nothing. But to his astonishment, Milgram found that rather than dismissing his students' fears, he was living them out. In a 1974 interview with *Psychology Today,* Milgram recalled how he approached his first person on the train:

"The words seemed lodged in my trachea and would simply not emerge."[21] It took him several unsuccessful attempts to get the first request out.

Despite the fact that people were more than willing to give up their seats or move over 68 percent of the time, this simple ask still elicited a major discomfort that, years later, his students recalled with visceral detail. Why was this such a painful experience? The internal voices of the participants in the experiment were likely screaming at them as they went onto the train:

You're going to die! This person is going to reject you and when you're rejected, you're kicked out of the tribe. Shamed.

You'll never make it out there on your own. You're going to die!!!!

Of course, the results were not nearly so dramatic. A simple "No" was the worst reaction. But that's not what tigers feel like to our brain. Rejection activates the same regions of the brain as physical pain, which is why we are so often paralyzed when it comes to making moves that might be really beneficial for us. But, in the short term, these also expose us to the serious discomfort of potential rejection or failure.[22] In order to "invite the tiger in for tea," we need to become more comfortable leaning into stressors we hadn't anticipated. Which means we need to practice.

Tiger Training:

STRESS INOCULATION

Just like athletes train to embrace physical discomfort as a key to their success (you have to literally rip your muscles for them to grow), so, too, must we endure a bit of physical, emotional, and mental discomfort to rebuild ourselves in order to use stress differently. Gains don't come easily, but a 2022 study of over two thousand people found that individuals willing to push themselves into awkward situations (i.e., taking improv classes) would later report the most personal growth.[23] Start small. No one gets up from the couch and goes out to run a three-hour marathon on the first day of training.

What's an easy, but slightly uncomfortable situation you could attempt to put yourself in?

Maybe you could try making eye contact with a stranger, and smile or say something complimentary about their outfit. Or, go knock on a neighbor's door requesting to borrow a cup of sugar, and return later with the cookies you baked. None of these suggestions get your heart rate racing? Try asking someone for their seat on the subway or bus, akin to Milgram's study, or perform some improv karaoke on the street corner.

If you need a list of other challenges, you can download more for free here:

Notice how you feel each time you go into your discomfort challenge. Feel the physiological rise—your heart pounding, mouth drying, sweat forming—and then lean into it. Don't try to calm down. Just run with it. You aren't facing tigers, and you're not going to die by asking to borrow someone's phone to make a quick call. These uncomfortable situations can be just like the stress your body endures on a 5k run—a heart-pumping, adrenaline-inducing ride—but each time you lean into this physiological rise, you train your brain to recognize that this feeling isn't life and death.

I often ask my audience to join me for some tiger training when I'm speaking. With their buy-in, I get people to their feet and then announce we are about to have a thirty-second dance party. There are usually a couple of cheers and a *lot* of groaning.

Can't we just do push-ups?

The rules for the dance party are simple:

1. There is no music (that would be far too comfortable)

   and

2. I need everyone to go ALL OUT. None of this two-stepping and clapping. I need *Seinfeld*'s Elaine's level of ALL-IN commitment.[24]

For thirty seconds, I ask people to get weird and boogie *hard*. From CEOs to sales teams, I've watched some of the greatest (and funkiest) dance moves in these thirty seconds of awkwardness. But, when the timer goes off, something funny always happens. People are smiling at one another. First off, it turns out that dancing in public isn't *actually* a tiger (although it might feel that way) and no one dies. But more to the point, everyone just went through the same discomfort *together*. When we endure challenges as a team, a company, a troop, a family, or a friend group, we end up closer as a result, and that's one heck of a powerful reason not to shy away from tigers. But how do we handle stress when the tiger finds us and we aren't actively seeking it? As much as tiger training can help us learn not to overreact to non–life-and-death situations of our choosing, our stress response will still be elicited from time to time by unexpected challenges.

Outrunning the Tiger

One of the first things to recognize when stress finds us (rather than us seeking discomfort), is that in those first three minutes of screaming terror, we will likely not respond logically. One of my favorite things to do with an audience is ask them to share with me their deepest, darkest fears. That ask is typically met with a silence so piercing, you can hear the hum of the lights. No one is about to voice their deepest, darkest fears in front of someone they just met (and a couple thousand of their closest friends and colleagues). But when I let the audience off the hook and ask people to guess the number-one fear of most Americans, they begin to perk up.

The responses vary a bit, but the following answers are consistent:

- *Rejection*
- *Failure*
- *Being alone*
- *Public speaking*
- *Death*

The funniest thing is that while none of these are the *actual* number-one fear, public speaking is usually rated higher on the list, making it more feared than death! (By this reasoning, the old Jerry Seinfeld joke that it's better to be in the casket than having to give the eulogy starts to make sense.)

Logically, our number-one fear should align with the number-one thing that ACTUALLY *kills us*—hamburgers and fries. Or something to that effect. Globally, the undisputed, number-one killer is heart disease.[25] But our brains persist in convincing us that we need supersized fries and sugar-loaded soda because these fats and sugars helped us survive in the harsh, food-scarce environments in which we evolved. Today, we play Russian roulette with our arteries every time we eat like this, but, as I stated at the start of this chapter, we don't act logically when our stress response is first initiated.

What is the *actual* number-one fear of Americans according to at least one survey?[26] Snakes. Snakes!? On paper, this is absurd. About five Americans die from venomous snake bites each year.[27] Compare this to the 2022 data showing that nearly 703,000 people die from heart disease each year in the United States, and the illogical stress response we have to snakes becomes even more blatant.[28] Want to feel even more foolish for our collective fear of snakes? The annual number of snake-related deaths is about the same as the number of people who die from having vending machines fall on them[29] or having a selfie-related fatal accident.[30]

Why the disconnect?

Because our brain isn't designed for logic—it's designed for survival. When our ancestors faced a snake, the ones who stopped to analyze the statistical probability of death didn't survive to become our ancestors. The ones who immediately jumped back? They passed on their genes.

We often struggle to control what we fear because it's baked so deeply into our instincts—instincts that were responsible for keeping us alive for 200,000–plus years (prior to the advent of selfies and vending machines). That's a lot of evolutionary time to try to quickly override when we're facing a harmless garter snake or attempting to be logical about a looming deadline. Both situations elicit an outsized, unhelpful stress response to situations that in the modern environment aren't actual life-and-death situations (not meeting the deadline probably doesn't mean you and your tribe will starve over the winter).

Our objective in this tiger stage is not to resist these instincts, but to invite in the flood of our stress physiology without resistance.

Stress and fear operate in the dark underworld of blackmail—they hold you hostage by promising to do that terrible thing you dread ("They'll reject you!"). But when you call their bluff, you stop draining your energy trying to avoid or blur or dampen the impact of your stress. You free yourself from being held hostage by first becoming aware of, and then actually feeling, the physiological effects of your stress. Our fears stay in control when our awareness of our emotions stays just out of reach. This is why fear pushes us toward distraction techniques like alcohol or drugs, or email and social media. These are easy habits to form in an attempt to avoid feeling the actual stress. But the more we try to avoid something, the more it can plague our thoughts, becoming repetitive and obsessive. Allow me to demonstrate. Try to not think about pink elephants right now. Whatever you do, don't envision a pink elephant riding a bicycle down the sidewalk. Stop it! Stop thinking about pink elephants!

See? The more we attempt to push our feelings of stress and fear back into some dark closet, the more likely they are to explode out at inconvenient times. Trying to "thought stop" actually redirects your attention to the very thought you are trying to avoid.[31] Here's the shift we need to make: Rather than trying to get rid of stress, invite the tiger in for a cup of tea and show yourself you don't actually need to fear it.

This invitation may take two forms:
PHYSICAL OR EMOTIONAL.

The setup looks the same for both: a safe space and a three-minute timer. When you feel the onset of the stressor, get to your safe space as quickly as possible. Set your timer for three minutes, then allow yourself to truly go deep into your stress and fear, feeling it all.

Your stress response is built for you to literally outrun a tiger.

Maybe that will mean a physical manifestation of the fear as you allow the energy to move through your body: screaming into a pillow, punching and kicking a weighted bag, or running hard on a treadmill.

Or, perhaps the stressor requires a more emotional outwitting of the tiger. In this case, try a free-flowing journal exercise and write openly, without interruption, about all of the disastrous things that will befall you, as well as your emotions as you experience them in the stress.

No matter which path you take, after three minutes, you will have either physically or mentally outrun the tiger. After those three minutes of screaming terror, your thoughts and feelings will begin moving from your limbic (the more primitive/reactionary portion of your brain) to your frontal lobe for deeper, more rational processing.

Another possible fun way to outrun the tiger—
SCREAM it away!

Try this:

All the problems we have with stress would end there if we were a zebra or a gazelle or if we were humans *actually* fighting for our lives. We'd want our blood pressure to be screaming upward and for our glucose to be released into our blood to feed the major muscles helping us flee or fight against our imminent death, and having now escaped, it should be over, right?

But the same program our body elicits to save us from tigers doesn't help us in the same way when we're sitting in traffic suffering from stress-induced hypertension, or when our body is signaling the need to replenish our glucose levels after a stressful meeting, causing us to sit at our desks snarfing down donuts and sweet tea having never actually run away from anything but our inbox. Closing a few tabs in our browser probably doesn't require us to replenish our blood sugar—but good luck convincing your body of that!

Unfortunately, most stress plagues us more long-term—well beyond those first three minutes of terror.

That's because humans have the unique gift (and curse) of turning on our stress response with thoughts, emotions, and memories. These thoughts can elicit the same physiological arousal as if the stressor were happening in the moment and send us careening in fear into both the past and future. We don't need that immediate surge of adrenaline that we get when we are startled, or when a stressor is acute, to keep our stress response turned on. Our thoughts and emotions can act just as effectively to punch the gas pedal of heightened threat. In chronic stress, the hypothalamic-pituitary-adrenocortical axis (or secondary stress network—a system that continues our heightened state after the short-lived adrenaline spike has faded) can remain in gear, revving up our system for far too long and causing damage if we don't mitigate it properly.[32] Once we recognize the threat is not a tiger, we can explore the true source and what else the stress might be signaling.

Stop Denying Yourself a Meaningful Life

I recently stumbled across some research I had read a few years before:

"People with very meaningful lives worry more and have more stress than people with less meaningful lives."

Wait, what?

I read it again.

To me, this was the most striking (and initially confusing!) finding from a 2013 study conducted by researchers at Stanford and Florida State University.[33] After analyzing the responses of nearly four hundred adults, those respondents who had experienced the greatest number of stressful life events in their past were also most likely to consider their life meaningful.

In fact, it wasn't just those who had experienced a high number of stressful life events in their past—every measure of stress the researchers asked about predicted a greater sense of meaning in life. Those who reported being under a lot of stress at the time of the study also rated their lives as more meaningful. The study even found that time spent worrying about the future was associated with a greater sense of meaning.

No wonder my grandmother, who wrung her hands at seemingly everything a person could possibly stress about, lived a long and, by all accounts (hers included), meaningful life.

WHAT IF WE ARE CHEATING OURSELVES OUT OF MEANING BY TRYING TO AVOID STRESS?

I'm not suggesting that we always need to find more stress in our lives. Goodness knows, we are all already suffering.

But this is why we suffer:

We are trying to control stress at this early stage through avoidance when it's often outside of our control.

We don't typically get asked if we want to have cancer or a new challenge at work. Certainly, one could argue that sometimes we do invite stress upon ourselves—a new baby perhaps, or a promotion—but even then, the stress we feel as a result isn't within our control (anyone who has been woken up at all hours of the night with a new child can attest to the lack of control). Rather than try to rid ourselves of the feeling of stress, what if instead we really allowed ourselves simply to feel it? To lean into the stressor rather than waste our energy trying to fight against something that, even if it was initially brought on with intention, is no longer ours to control? Suffering occurs when we fight a stressor's presence in our life. Rather, we should attempt to accept and invite the stress in, even if reluctantly. Maybe we can even start running toward it!

Run to the Roar

What would happen if rather than trying to avoid our stress, we run right toward it? Meet up with our stress in the spots we most fear going. Sound crazy? Again, I'm not suggesting you look for an awful diagnosis or hope for some other horrible circumstance, but rather than try to tamp down or be rid of all the stressors, what would happen if you found a way to use them? Our culture is rich with examples of people we celebrate for running directly toward the roars of their tigers. Michael Jordan had a deep fear of failure and rejection after he was cut from his high school basketball team. Rather than allowing this fear to paralyze him, he used it as motivation to work harder than ever. In his famous words, "I've failed over and over and over again in my life. And that is why I succeed." As he's now a six-time NBA champion and a cultural icon, I'd say things worked out alright for the guy.

Jordan understood:

FAILURE ≠ TIGER.

Perhaps my favorite example of how running toward the roar can change not only one person's life, but the history of an entire country, is the renowned orator and leader, former US President Theodore "Teddy" Roosevelt. Early in life, Roosevelt suffered from debilitating shyness and a fear of public speaking.[34] Rather than run away from them, Roosevelt decided to confront his fears head-on, joining the Harvard debate club and finding other outlets to force himself to speak publicly as often as possible. By using his fear rather than fighting it, he tamed his tiger and from it, went on to produce some of the most powerful, bold, roars of speeches Americans had ever heard. The crux of all his work comes to the forefront for me in "The Man in the Arena" address, which emphasizes the value of action, courage, and perseverance in the face of criticism and adversity. In this meta moment of power, Roosevelt argues that the real credit belongs to those who strive boldly despite their imperfections or the possibility of failure, rather than to the critics who sit on the sidelines and judge.

Here's the key passage:

It is not the critic who counts; not the man who points out how the strong man stumbles, or where the doer of deeds could have done them better. The credit belongs to the man who is actually in the arena, whose face is marred by dust and sweat and blood; who strives valiantly; who errs, who comes short again and again, because there is no effort without error and shortcoming; but who does actually strive to do the deeds; who knows great enthusiasms, the great devotions; who spends himself in a worthy cause; who at the best knows in the end the triumph of high achievement, and who at the worst, if he fails, at least fails while daring greatly, so that his place shall never be with those cold and timid souls who neither know victory nor defeat.[35]

YOU'RE STRAPPED INTO THIS ROLLER COASTER OF LIFE.

You are already in the arena. Rather than seek shelter and escape, why not embrace those tigers in front of you and find out what you can do together?

If this all still feels a little backward, I'll invite you to participate in some follow-up research I conducted on the heels of reading the 2013 study on how stressful lives were highly correlated to meaningful ones. I asked over five thousand people to think about a project or an accomplishment that they were most proud of. Once they had that project in mind, I invited them to go back in time to when they were in the middle of that project and assess their levels of stress.

On a scale of 0–100, how stressed would you have rated yourself?

Bingo.

Help us collect more data by submitting your answer here:

If you participated in answering the previously posed question, the results are likely unsurprising to you. About 4 percent of people responded that they had little to no stress while accomplishing their most important project.

To these people, I want to say,

GET BIGGER GOALS!

Another 23 percent of people reported that they had a moderate amount of stress. According to the traditional Yerkes-Dodson model, these 23 percent would have fallen perfectly in their zone of optimal performance. But that would mean that the vast majority (73 percent of us, including several outliers that I had to remove for reporting scores well above 100) reported that our stress levels were way above our optimal range. We were stressed out of our gourds while we were in the middle of these projects! And yet, these are the projects and the accomplishments around which we have the most pride.

This is what brings meaning to our lives. We are already using stress to springboard us whether or not we're doing it intentionally. The goal now is to be able to use this springboard in real time, rather than only retrospectively recognizing its power.

Rather than fight the tiger and suffer through these projects and experiences, embrace the stress, whether you have brought it upon yourself or it found you. Stop trying to control that initial fear and recognize that this stressor isn't a tiger. Go ahead and kick and yell and run and do whatever you need to do for the first three minutes of screaming terror.

But if you've survived, if you're still alive three minutes after the stressor hits (or the thought of the stressor arises), you get the opportunity to play a new game, one in which you can begin channeling your stress into action. It requires bravery and courage to take ownership of the ride, to raise your hand and volunteer for it, or even to accept what you can't control when the anxiety-provoking stressors of your life find you without an invitation. But without tackling it head-on, this stress can seep into your very self and erode you from the inside out. When you are willing to look closer, to recognize that the stressor you face is not a tiger, you can be the one to extend the invitation—to adventure, to challenge, to a new opportunity.

The ultimate power isn't in avoiding stress—it's in inviting it in and saying, "Thank you for this energy. Now, let me show you what I can do with it."

In the next chapter, I'll show you exactly how to transfer this energy into unstoppable momentum.

It's time to move to the
FEAR[less] STAGE.

Chapter 5

Choose Your Own Adventure

"The greatest weapon against stress is our ability to choose one thought over another."
—**William James**

Objectives:
1. **Feel stress in a new way. Rather than triggering fear or anxiety, how can experiencing stress be a moment of excitement?**
2. **Keep the energy of stress high, but begin to challenge its meaning.**

A dear friend of mine has been trying to have a family for years. After the devastating realization that she couldn't biologically conceive, she and her husband turned to adoption. They filled out mountains of paperwork and endured multiple mandatory home inspections. Together, they executed fundraisers and threw galas to raise the money they needed to cover the surprisingly expensive process. But waiting turned out to be the hardest part.

An estimated two million couples are currently waiting to adopt in the United States, and wait times often extend to years.[36]

Normally, when I arrive at my friend's house, she'll greet me at the door moments after I ring the doorbell, but on this particular day, as I pulled up to her house, she didn't wait for me to reach her doorstep. Flinging her door open, she bounded out of the house and across the lawn, yelling something that took my brain a moment to process.

"We have a baby!
We got a baby!!
Two, actually! Twins!!"

From the moment she had begun running toward me, my heart rate had increased. I could feel my breathing quicken. Every hair on my arms had come up to attention. Known scientifically as "piloerection," my goose bumps were a subconscious, autonomic physiological response to an unknown something, something I had to prepare for, like a dog raising its hackles (admittedly a bit of an absurd defense for us humans these days, given how little hair we have left on our bodies). I was in a heightened state—a kind of emotional purgatory where my brain hadn't yet processed what was happening, but my body was prepared to react to whatever positive or negative thing awaited.

When my brain finally caught up to what she was saying—*A baby! They had gotten a child!*—I burst into a huge grin, and tears streamed down my face. My heart rate didn't change. My breathing stayed quick.

When we describe emotions, they are often referenced using two descriptive dimensions:[37]

1. **Arousal:** Arousal refers to the level of activation, energy, or intensity associated with an emotion. It indicates how calming or stimulating an emotion is, and can range from low arousal (calm, relaxed) to high arousal (excited, anxious). For instance, emotions like calmness and contentment are low in arousal, while emotions like fear and anger are high in arousal.

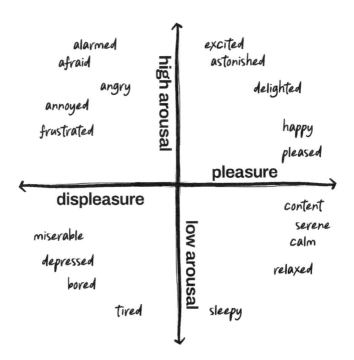

2. **Valence:** Valence refers to the positivity or negativity of the emotion. Emotions can be categorized along a spectrum ranging from positive to negative. For example, joy, love, and excitement are considered positive emotions, while sadness, fear, and anger are considered negative emotions. Emotional valence helps us to understand whether an emotion is pleasant or unpleasant.

It's important to note that arousal and valence are processed in different parts of the brain.[38] As my friend was running at me from her front door, I moved immediately into a high-arousal state without the ability to yet label the emotional valence. Was her rushing out to see me a good thing or a bad thing? I hadn't yet decided, and that's where the opportunity for us lies. We might not get to choose how our body responds to arousal (our heart pumping, our hair standing on end), but we do have some say in the interpretation of the emotional valence.

Later that day, I thought to look at the data from my WHOOP band that I wear to track my activity level. You can see the two times during the day that my band had detected known activities. I had taken a short walk prior to lunch, and then did a very quick weight lifting session after lunch before driving out to my friend's house. I pulled up to her doorstep at 2:00 p.m.

For a solid fifteen minutes, I was in what the data would show to be a high-stress zone.

And I was.

This is the magic of the stress response. It's not good or bad—it's just high arousal. Stress doesn't give us the valence of the emotion. It's how we interpret the stress energy that matters, and that happens later and separate from the experience of the high arousal. Had my friend come to me that day in the same manner but delivered horrible news, my WHOOP data would have likely looked the same. This injudiciousness of the stress response to delegate any particular valence of emotion (pleasant or unpleasant) gives us an incredible opportunity to truly use stress to our advantage.

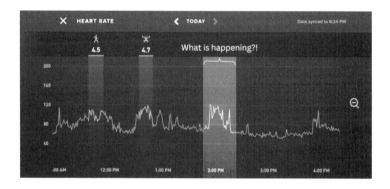

What I was experiencing when my friend came careening out to meet me to share her great news with me was stress: a high-arousal level. But I didn't experience it as negative stress because, as my friend shared her news, my mind interpreted it as something different: **excitement.**

EXCITEMENT = HIGH AROUSAL + POSITIVE VALENCE.

In this case, my brain made the switch easily and naturally transferred all of that stress energy into excitement because the news I received had such a positive valence.

BUT WHAT IF YOU'RE HEARING NEWS THAT ISN'T NECESSARILY AS GOOD?

Maybe it's news that strikes fear into your heart.

Let's try this scenario:

Imagine that you work in a large organization. Tomorrow is the annual conference, and you've been slotted to give the opening keynote in front of the whole company, including your boss, the CEO, and the board. All of your colleagues will be there, and your family has been invited to sit at the front honorary table. What advice would you give yourself?

If you responded, "try to calm down," you're among the vast majority of people. According to a 2013 study, about 91 percent of participants given a similar scenario suggested that they would advise themselves to try to relax or calm down.[39] (Although I'm partial to the 2 percent of people who suggested that they try to weasel out of the speech or find someone else to do it altogether!) But, even though the "Keep Calm and Carry On" 1939 British propaganda slogan is having a revitalization moment, the advice turns out to be outdated at best. At worst, trying to stay calm when you're feeling anxious might actually have detrimental results.

No one in the history of feeling stressed has ever stressed less when they are told to "just calm down."

When we're told to calm down while we're in an anxious state, we often react negatively or defensively because calming yourself simply isn't biologically possible when you're in a high-arousal state. You cannot will your heart to beat slower or your adrenaline not to be released from your adrenal glands. Hence, the command to "calm down" can make people feel defensive, frustrated, or deficient, fueling the heightened state of arousal and having the exact opposite effect from the intended "calming." And it doesn't seem to matter if the voice telling you to "calm down" is someone else or your own internal voice: Either way, the result is often a magnification or amplification of the stress—not its intended diminishment.

That's because your whole body is tingling with energy, and energy cannot be destroyed, or in this case, stuffed away. It must be transferred. Think back to your high school physics class. The law of conservation states that energy cannot be created or destroyed, but it can change forms. Energy can transform from potential to kinetic or, in our case, from anxious and erratic to useful and actionable.

Imagine your autonomic nervous system, the network of nerves in your body that controls all the processes that upregulate or downregulate your systems unconsciously—heart rate, blood pressure, etc.—as a simple continuum from deep sleep to your highest state of alertness (deep fear or maximal excitement).

When we're nervous or anxious, even though we've made the choice that the stressor is not a tiger, our body is still on that higher end of the continuum—buzzing with energy. The cool thing is that stress, fear, and several other emotions like excitement, anger, and astonishment are experienced quite similarly in the body. Each of these high-arousal emotions elicits similar hormones, so our bodies prepare for both anxiety and excitement with a nearly identical physiological response. The hormones we produce during low-arousal events are quite different, however, which is why being told to calm down when you're in a heightened, autonomic state isn't helpful.

BUT THERE *IS* A SHIFT THAT GIVES US BACK OUR POWER IN THESE MOMENTS.

Staying in that same heightened physiological state (not trying to "destroy" our energy), we can decide that our feelings of stress and fear are actually other emotions that have a similar arousal profile. This is sometimes referred to as *emotional reappraising,* and is, in essence, a reinterpretation of the feelings we initially associate with that heightened state. Reappraisal is a key component in treatments for anxiety and mood disorders and has been used to improve emotional regulation, lower negative emotions, increase positive emotions, and even improve cardiovascular and cognitive responses to stress.

This is the power move.
You can choose to fear less.

With practice, we can begin assigning a more positive emotional valence to the stressor immediately, never having to convince ourselves to move, for example, from fear to excitement, but rather being excited from the start of that physiological rise. Now, if you're like me and thinking, "That sounds ridiculous, I can't just shift my feelings of anxiety to excitement," I hear you. And in some respects, you're right. Once activated, an aroused state is difficult to control, so shifting feelings from anxiety to *calm* is next to impossible. But in this case, we aren't trying to change the physiological signals happening in our bodies (increased heart rate, rapid breathing, etc.); we are simply leaning into the interpretation of those feelings differently at the same heightened arousal state. Rather than trying to force a less-aroused state, we are reinterpreting our body's signals in a positive way that can enhance our performance rather than debilitate it.

Interpreting Stress as Enhancing

When we see stress as enhancing, we're more likely to stay motivated and focused, build competence, and integrate lessons such that we're more prepared for future stressors. The way we interpret our stress energy even has significant implications for our longevity and health.

A 2012 study asked the following questions to thirty thousand people across the United States:[40]

1. How much stress have you experienced in the last year?

2. Do you believe that stress is harmful for your health?

The researchers then tracked who, among those people, died over the next eight years. Bad news first: People with the highest level of stress increased their risk of death by 43 percent; that might not be surprising to most of us that nod in agreement because we've all heard how dangerous and bad stress can be.

But here's the kicker: This high mortality was only linked to those people who had high levels of stress and who also believed that stress was harmful to their health. People who experienced the same high levels of stress but didn't view it as harmful to their health were actually less likely to die than those people who reported relatively little stress in their lives.

Based on these percentages, researchers estimated that over the course of the eight-year study, approximately 182,000 Americans died prematurely, not from stress, but from the *belief* that stress was bad for them. That's over 20,000 deaths per year, which, to put it into perspective, is more than double the number of Americans that died of skin cancer in 2024.[41]

So, what's your stress mindset?

- **Is it that stress is enhancing?** *My physiological response is generating courage and preparing my body to meet a challenge by mobilizing energy.*

  or

- **Is it that stress is debilitating?** *I must calm down because my physiological response is demonstrating that I'm in a threatening situation. I'm not handling the situation well. Now I'm sweating and my body is starting to betray me . . . EEEK!*

Most of us, myself included, have been taught the latter. When I first read the aforementioned study, I immediately began to stress about how I could possibly change my stress mindset as quickly as possible.

I was like the cowardly lion from *The Wizard of Oz,* panicking after seeing his friend the Tin Man mysteriously lifted into the air in the haunted forest.

"I do believe in spooks, I do believe in spooks!"

"I do believe stress is enhancing, it does help me, it does, it does, it does!"

And as it turns out, that affirmation might just be enough to cognitively control our responses to stress: to show *mind over matter.*

Mind over Matter

In a study cleverly titled "Mind over Matter: Reappraising Arousal Improves Cardiovascular and Cognitive Responses to Stress," participants were asked to think about their bodily response to stress as functional and adaptive (i.e., *My heart is pumping oxygen faster to my brain for quick processing.*).[42] The results demonstrated that the cardiovascular functioning of participants improved, and they exhibited less threat-related attentional bias even under stressful conditions. In other words, they were primed to find adventure and opportunity rather than be afraid of a charging tiger on the horizon.

When we shift from interpreting our bodily response to stress from feelings of fear to feelings of excitement, or at least to acknowledging that those feelings can serve us, we move toward being able to take advantage of stress rather than staying hidden in the shadows, trying to avoid it. This action gives us a sense of autonomy and control over the situation, even if the stressor is not something we would have chosen. It mobilizes the energy we need as we embark on our adventure and face unknown circumstances.

The Transfer (ANXIETY to Excitement)

Hang out around any United States Marine Corps training grounds, and you'll surely hear the grunts and echoes of the OORAH battle cry. While the origins of the call are hotly debated, the consensus seems to land on its 1953 genesis in a recon unit deployed off the shores of Korea.[43] Marines aboard the submarines in the 1st Amphibious Reconnaissance Company would hear the distinct call of a Klaxon alarm *(Aarugha!)* as they submerged. While an alarm is obviously meant to signal, well, alarm, apparently after observing how these sailors responded to the *arrruuggghhhaaaa*, Marines began to use the sound to motivate one another during training exercises. *OORAH* was the simplified version that eventually arose and today still carries the same energy and excitement as those original Klaxon alarms.

Listen to the alarms here:

According to Marine Cam Beck, the *OORAH* cry can signal one of at least ten things.[44] In each interpretation, you'll be able to see the transfer of anxiety, fear, and uncertainty into a more controlled state of excitement, comradery, and awe.

The interpretation of OORAH might mean:

1. I am a Marine.

2. I enthusiastically accept your message.

3. I am excited to be here.

4. Pleased to make your acquaintance.

5. What you ask of me, not only will I do, but I will also do in a manner befitting a Marine.

6. I expect good things from you.

7. Good job.

8. I am not supposed to be motivated about performing this task, but I will force myself to express excitement for the benefit of my fellow Marines and to tactfully annoy my superiors who gave me the task.

9. I love being a Marine.

10. I am about to destroy something.

While we civilians may not be hearing sirens or be asked to summon courage and excitement for a dangerous mission or physically demanding task, most people experience anxiety many times each day,[45] with negative effects on cognition,[46] performance, and motivation.[47] Rather than focusing on the task at hand, people experiencing anxiety will waste working memory on worry and rumination, and even stress about the fact that they are stressed![48] And our own research suggests that people stress out *more* when they're trying not to stress about their stress!

Most Americans in our 2024 research study indicated that they were stressing out about trying to control their stress. The more anxious people become, the less they believe they can succeed, which lowers self-confidence and profoundly impacts decision-making and behavior. Talk about a losing downward spiral!

For example, when negotiating, people who are in an anxious state make low first offers, exit early, and earn less profit than neutral-state negotiators, self-handicapping themselves for future opportunities in the process.[49] And our research found that when stressed, 58 percent of Americans reduce their self-care, lowering their overall sense of well-being and contributing to— you guessed it—*more stress.*

So, what should we do with all this stress energy so that it doesn't leave us feeling scatterbrained, demotivated, self-doubting, and on a negative spiral?

We need to transfer it into energy that serves us, helps us mount an adaptive response, and propels us toward a desirable outcome. We need to take the fear out of the stress. Sometimes, that might be as simple as responding with a forcefully enthusiastic *OORAH!*

"Let's get after it. Those things I just heard about strike fear into my heart, but OORAH! I'm ready. Let's go!"

That drilled-in Marine response to challenge is there for a reason. It's a perfect example of transferring anxious energy into positive action by exclaiming something akin to, *I'm excited!* But how do we use this in our everyday lives to increase performance with things we really aren't excited about?

Let's return for a moment to that public speaking challenge I referenced earlier, where you've been asked to give the opening keynote to your large organization. In 2013, a study from Harvard Business School explored a similar exercise.[50] One hundred and forty participants were given two minutes to prepare a speech to persuade an experimenter that they would make a good work partner. The participants were informed that they would deliver the speech in front of the researcher, who would capture the speech on video so that it could later be judged by a committee of peers. Just before delivering their speeches, participants were randomly assigned to two groups. The first group was asked to make the statement "I am calm" just before delivering their speech to the camera. The second group made the statement "I am excited" under the same conditions.

Independent raters who later watched each speech (without hearing the "I am excited" or "I am calm" preliminary statements) rated the participants from both groups, and the results were mind-blowing.

Participants who stated **"I am excited"** before giving their speech were rated as significantly more persuasive, more competent, more confident, and more persistent than the participants who stated **"I am calm"** before the camera started rolling.

Fascinatingly, there was no significant difference in how participants in either group were rated on their level of anxiety or excitement. Perhaps that's because self-reported anxiety did not differ significantly between the groups. In other words, participants who were asked to say "I am excited" still felt anxious, but despite their feelings, that simple statement of excitement was enough to significantly increase their performance across multiple measures. Their nervous energy had been converted into useful fuel in the form of excitement.

So, if you are, like me, in the skeptical camp that believes you can't force yourself into feeling something different, you're right. At least in part.

These participants didn't feel any changes in their level of anxiety, but independent of how they felt, their performance benefited significantly.

I often have some fun with audiences when I'm speaking about transferring energy. I'll walk up on stage, hunched over, clutching the sides of my pants and playing with them nervously. Then, as I look at the ground, I'll say flatly and softly, "I'm so excited to be with you all today." As you might imagine, the audience doesn't really know what to make of this. A lot of people begin shifting in their seats uncomfortably, nervous due to my own apparent anxiety.

Because we are a social species, we've evolved a way to pick up signals from others and connect with people on an emotional level. We have special neurons in our brains called mirror neurons that help us detect and reflect back the emotions of others.[51] It's why contagious giggles happen (or contagious fear and stress responses, for that matter). Our brain subconsciously picks up signals from others, and in an effort to connect with those people on an emotional level, *will alter our own emotional state to be more reflective of theirs.* Emotional contagion is powerful, so when, for example, I show up on stage "nervous," others meet me where I am, and feed that back to me. The result is a downward spiral of nerves, our anxiety feeding on one another's emotional state.

But what happens when, even in a moment of elevated arousal, I instead throw my shoulders back, lift my head in pride, and meet the eyes of the audience with a confident greeting? The same mirror neurons of their excitement and anticipation can spur me forward in my own feigned confidence, transforming it into actual excitement.

SIMPLY STATING "I'M EXCITED" OR ACTING AS IF YOU ARE WHEN YOU FEEL STRESSED OR ANXIOUS MAKES A HUGE DIFFERENCE.

Deliberately misrepresenting anxious arousal as excitement (even if you don't fully believe it yourself) leads to increased feelings of excitement and to improved performance (again, even if your anxiety levels don't actually decrease). In part, that's the result of the environmental and social feedback we receive, but it's also in equal part the result of changing our internal feedback mechanisms.

That's because the things we do influence how we feel.

Actions affect feelings, which is counterintuitive to how we typically think. We don't smile because we're happy; we're happy because we smile. Known as *somatic feedback*, our emotions are a product of or a response to our actions—not the other way around. Our brain is scanning our body to understand how it should interpret the rush of neurotransmitters and hormones it's experiencing. Are we slouched over and drawn into ourselves *(Yikes, this must be something scary!),* or are we open chested with our shoulders drawn back *(Oooh, we must be excited about this!)*?

In a fascinating experiment conducted by researchers at Columbia University, participants were shown video clips designed to evoke positive or negative emotions (such as *America's Funniest Home Videos or Fear Factor*).[52] Just prior to watching the videos, participants in one group received Botox (which paralyzes facial muscles), while others received Restylane (a cosmetic filler that doesn't affect facial muscles). After watching the videos, those who received Botox reported a significant decrease in emotional intensity compared to the Restylane group. The mild facial paralysis was enough to dampen emotional responses, and the brains of the participants didn't react as dramatically to the inputs.

A similar experiment made famous by psychologist Daniel Kahneman asked students to hold a pencil horizontally between their teeth without their lips touching the pencil, essentially forcing a smile.[53] The students in this condition reported cartoons to be funnier and a greater overall sense of happiness during the experiment relative to the control group. As Kahneman quipped in his book *Thinking, Fast and Slow,* "Being amused tends to make you smile, and smiling tends to make you feel amused." We forget that our brain is completely reliant on external cues to interpret signals inside the body. Is that feeling excitement or anxiety?

A SMILE INDICATES EXCITEMENT, AND THAT SOMATIC FEEDBACK SIGNALS TO OUR BRAIN THAT WE ARE SAFE.

In the same vein, it's likely you've heard of Power Poses, **as Amy Cuddy's TED Talk on the topic has garnered over 73 million views, and counting!**[54]

Her work has demonstrated that merely adopting a pose you feel is powerful—a Wonder Woman stance, for instance—can dramatically affect your confidence and your actual performance through hormonally mediated changes in the body. In other words, your positioning of your body (not just your facial expressions) signals to your brain via hormones what the situation at hand really is.

All the attention drew a lot of criticism to Cuddy's work, but an extensive meta-analysis on the seventy-three published studies on power posing done in 2020 seems to have finally put the debate to rest.[55] Get ready to strike a pose, because this stuff works.

When comparing open or expansive poses (think Wonder Woman or Superman, or a boss with her feet up on the desk) to closed poses (hunched over at a desk, or crossed arms and a downcast gaze), the researchers found robust effects for changes in both behavior and mood. And in many cases, they could observe beneficial shifts in underlying hormonal chemistry for those that power-posed for even sixty seconds before a stressful or high-stakes encounter.

Whether we're power-posing, chomping on pencils, shouting *OORAH*, or simply stating "I'm excited!" the results are consistent and convincing. Scoring higher, with greater accuracy, and performing at your best doesn't mean trying to decrease feelings of anxiety, as we've been taught. The arousal state is fixed. Rather, it's the transference of that energy into excitement about the task and the changing of your emotional valence that makes the difference.

But what about those moments when a statement of excitement just doesn't cut it (for example, a terminal diagnosis of a partner)?

The Case for ANGER

In these cases, anger might be another viable high-arousal emotion that can be useful in reappraisal. Again, we aren't trying to calm down but rather to embrace the full energy arousal to motivate and mobilize ourselves against the challenge. Anger prepares you in the same way as excitement with a readiness for action. Studies have found that becoming angry can increase our effort toward attaining a desired goal and frequently results in greater success.[56]

A burst of anger can also spark greater creativity.[57] People who are primed to be in a high-arousal state like anger are more original and come up with more varied solutions in brainstorming activities than those who are in a more neutral or calm state (yet another argument against trying to tamp down your physiological response to a challenge!).

I'll often use anger as a motivator for creative problem-solving during workshops. Too often, we point anger in the wrong direction, toward an opponent rather than at the problem we need to solve (more on the importance of choosing your trajectory well in the coming chapter). One example I use frequently involves one of the most divisive issues in our nation: gun control. Any audience will typically contain the full spectrum of ideologies, from those who strictly oppose any infringement on their right to bear arms of any kind to those who would have all guns removed from society if possible. The anger on both sides of the issue can feel palpable. The trick is using it productively. Here's what I argue that everyone in the audience can agree on: *Our kids shouldn't be dying from gun violence in schools.* The fact that this is happening **should** anger everyone. The resulting brainstorm for how to prevent this issue is always a flurry of productive and cooperative solutions from all sides.

When we reappraise stress energy as excitement or anger, or even as simply adaptive and ready to serve us, we take the first step toward resolving the issue rather than avoiding it.

STRESS
IS SIMPLY OUR BODY'S ADAPTIVE RESPONSE TO SOLVING A PROBLEM.

The difference between staying in fear and finding power in our stress by fearing less is a subtle shift in how we register the emotional valence of the arousal state. The only question left then is, how do we best use the energy we've harnessed?

And that is the final step in the FEAR[less] Stress Formula:

The Springboard.

The fastest way to engage in this step of the FEAR[less] Stress Formula is to act

"as if."

Rather than "faking it until you make it," acting "as if" adopts the mindset that you are already excited! Feel your heart racing? Don't deny your anxiety or stress, but work to acknowledge and transfer its energy by telling yourself that it's launching you off that Yerkes-Dodson curve to your highest performance. You are excited or angry. You choose. Then express it. In your facial expressions, your clenched fists, in your words to yourself or others around you, in your body language. Remind yourself that the way your body is responding enhances your ability to rise to the challenge. You're primed for an opportunity mindset and ready to point all your motivation and energy into your performance.

Let's gooooooooooo!!

Chapter 6

Springboarding Toward Action

Objectives:

1. Channel the energy of excitement or anger into a productive path of micro-goals that point toward a higher purpose.
2. Align yourself in the broader context of community.

Driving Toward Action

A few years ago, I had the opportunity to go to a local track to race cars with my husband. Now, let me be clear with you, I am not a race car driver.

This is my husband's hobby and one he's quite talented in, so I figured I'd tag along and see what I could do. I had a goal, though: I wanted to beat him on just one lap. I listened intently to the instructors—slow into the curves, accelerate out. I understood the principles, and strapping into my car, I was excited to put them into practice. A few laps in, I began to feel confident. I was, after all, representing my entire gender out there on the track that day, so I was ready to show everyone what I could do. Turn three was coming up, and my husband was just in front of me. I mentally prepared to make the pass.

Slow into the curve, accelerate out, and blow right by him!

See the actual footage of me making the pass attempt here:

My heart was pounding, my nostrils flared with the exhaust of his car just in front of me. I hit the accelerator hard . . . and immediately felt my car begin to spin around before coming to a bumpy stop off the track just before the wall. I sat for a minute to gather myself before a scream of frustration came to my lips. The tow truck came to pull my car out of the grass and over to the pit station to be fixed up. I sat helplessly in the driver's seat, being dragged behind the truck with tears welling up in my eyes. Hot tears. Shame tears. Tears of anger.

I was solidly in my three minutes of screaming terror. After I got out of my still-smoking car, the instructor came up beside me and leaned against the fence post where I stood, helmet still on, trying to conceal my embarrassment.

"You know, Beck," he started, staring at the track in an attempt to spare me from complete humiliation, "there are really two types of drivers out there. There are drivers like your husband, and he's pretty good!"

At this point I could feel the swell of anger in my body. I just wanted to bolt. I did not want to hear this. I was stuck in a place of fear, in the binary thinking that our brain falls into when we haven't yet invited the tiger in or transferred the stress energy. I was in full-on comparison mode, thinking, *Oh, he's good, therefore I must be lousy. He's successful, therefore I must be a failure.*

But then the instructor continued, "Yeah, your husband is good . . . but he's never going to be great."

Say what?

He had my full attention.

MY BRAIN FLIPPED . . .
TO CURIOSITY.

How was my husband not great? Did this give me a chance to win?

"He's never going to be great until he does the thing you just did there about six thousand more times. Until he pushes that car faster than he knows it can go and spins out again and again, he won't find his not-yet moment."

Data. The instructor was talking about trajectories—small, actionable steps forward, regardless of the immediate outcome.

I had failed. Good!

That meant I now had data. I had the opportunity to go out again more prepared as a result. Maybe, just maybe, I was the good kind of driver he had referenced.

The instructor shook his head and gave a sly smile. "Drivers like you, Beck, they usually quit." And with that, he strolled away.

Quit. Yes, that's exactly what I wanted to do. I wanted to control my outcome, and the only way I could be certain of that outcome was to not get back in the car. Not risk another spin out, another embarrassment.

We humans are really good at measuring, anticipating even, the costs of our actions—our failures, screwups, and spinouts. But often, we do not consider measuring the total cost of our inactions. I could have put-putted behind my husband all day on the track and never spun out and avoided the embarrassment to begin with, but how would I have felt when I got home, having never tried to pass my husband?

Meh. Okay. Fine.

How would I feel if I spent the rest of the day watching, rather than getting back in the car? Meh. Okay. Fine.

I'D HAVE BEEN SAFE. I'D HAVE BEEN IN CONTROL OF THE OUTCOME.

But I'd have ignored the real threat that would come to haunt me later. The real cost of playing it safe.

If I didn't get back into the car that day, I would have had to lie in bed that night listening to the sirens of regret play on repeat in my head.

Why hadn't I tried? Why didn't I use my new knowledge? Why didn't I . . . Speak up? Stand out? Raise my hand? Nominate myself? Why didn't I set the example that the next young girl needed?

I got back in the car. I spun out two more times that day. Did I reach my goal of beating my husband? **No.** But did I inch my way closer every time I got back in the car?

Absolutely.

The only way to stay in complete control of the outcome is by not taking steps that get you closer to your goal. Making binary, fear-based choices—*I win or nothing*—does not provide a path forward. Ironically, that type of thinking is the biggest thing holding us back from getting closer to the win. It ensures we play it safe. We exist our way through life, put-putting behind our fullest potential rather than risk inviting the tiger into the arena with us and using our stress energy to inch us toward new heights.

How can we begin to point ourselves practically toward trajectories that bring us fully into our highest potential?

First, we need to know what to avoid.

Springboarding Without Alignment

Your energy needs direction. We've all had the experience of an angry boss or partner. They're upset about an issue that we may or may not have been a part of, but all the anger and frustration comes barreling down on us in the form of blame and finger-pointing. Or maybe we do this to ourselves by internalizing our own anger. If we don't focus on the trajectory of our energy, rather than creatively solving the problem, our stress energy often gets unloaded in unhealthy patterns.

Think about your last argument with your spouse or colleague. Were you fighting the problem, the obstacle, or were you fighting one another? If you fought the problem, even if you were in heated debate about the best approach, you likely came out stronger, with a better relationship. At least, that's what a multitude of studies are reporting about using anger well. Anger, with a trajectory toward a common enemy or problem, increases people's sense of control. But without that alignment, things can easily spin out of control (or grind to a standstill).

At the beginning of this book, I shared a story about the month when I quit my job, sold my house, and divorced my husband. While it may have felt brave or bold at the time, I was acting out of fear even then. Fear doesn't allow us to point toward a specific trajectory or pathway. Its springboard launches us broadly into the territory of **"anything but . . . "** Anything but failure or loneliness or rejection, which can leave us bouncing up and down with no path forward.

Here, our fear will say:

- *Run away.*

- *Don't show up.*

- *Don't give it your all.*

- *Give yourself wiggle room for an excuse for why you didn't really go all in with your efforts.*

The first time I distinctly remember allowing my fear to steer me was when I was eight.

I loved being in the spotlight even then and had joined my local 4-H club to enter public speaking competitions. I had won at my local and county levels, meaning I'd qualified for state competition. State competition! It felt like a huge deal. It wasn't just my parents who knew about my speech; it was my friends, my teachers, my instructors for band, choir, and theater, and my older sister (my role model and hero) who pulled me aside and told me she was betting on me. Betting on me! I was feeling the pressure. My worlds were colliding and funneling into what felt like my big shot. I did not want to blow it for myself, but most notably, I didn't want to blow it for anyone else. I didn't want to prove myself unworthy. More than anything, I did not want to fail. My springboard was loaded, but it wasn't pointed anywhere.

After all my preparation,

(yes, I can still give the opening line of that talk to this day.)

and hard work,

**when the
day of the
competition
rolled around…**

I never showed up.

I played sick.

I didn't get back in the car.
(Shoot, I never got in the car to begin with!)

My fear was steering me, not toward any goal or possibility, but rather away from any exposure or liability, any possibility that anyone would see me as a failure.

- *Where are you playing sick right now?*
- *Where are you playing it safe?*

Where are you not going all in because you're listening to that little voice in your head, that fear, that says, *Maybe it's better to hold back this time and not risk exposing yourself as a failure?*

So many of us have spent years listening to that voice. Courting or marrying the wrong person, or spending thousands of dollars obtaining a degree we don't really want, fearing we won't be enough without it, and it's all to avoid potential negative outcomes that are mostly in our own heads.

But what if instead, we used all that energy we've now converted to point toward a new pathway, a job we might actually enjoy or a risk we take for love?

The springboard can give you the energy and drive to work through the difficult issues and sort out how to start on that pathway.

Steering with Curiosity & the Cost of Inaction

In order to set a trajectory forward, our first step is simply to get curious.

- *Where do you want to go?*
- *What do you want to accomplish?*
- *Where do you want to point all of that transferred stress energy to enhance your performance?*
- *How will you invest that excitement? That anger?*
- *Why does it matter that you do?*

CURIOSITY AND FEAR CANNOT COEXIST.
Let me repeat that, because it is so fundamentally important. Curiosity and fear cannot coexist.

There is no brain mechanism for it. For more than two hundred thousand years of our ancestry, no human has ever had a tiger charging them and thought, *Huh, I wonder how fast it's moving?* As a result, if, in our excitement and heightened arousal state, we can get curious, we can further distance ourselves from fear. We can begin to channel our emotions into a laser focus on moving forward. Rather than be enslaved to our threat physiology, feeling chaotic, out of control, and without direction, we start aligning our energies toward positive action.

With curiosity, we can begin to steer our excitement or anger into productive outcomes (i.e., I want to . . . solve this problem, be with this person, perform at this higher level, etc.). When we get curious, we put ourselves into a state of approach. In other words, we are more motivated to move *toward* something in our environment when we are in that highly aroused state, rather than simply avoiding it or running away.

The challenge here is to move in that direction *independent* of the outcome. Setting a trajectory is not the same as setting an outcome goal. An outcome goal is finite, is not necessarily within our direct control, and is typically separated by some distance in time. Outcome goals are often the very things that spark the most fear and "playing sick." My eight-year-old outcome goal was to win that state competition. That's a goal that was outside of my control. I had no control over whether or not the other competitors would be better than me or if the judges would have a soft spot for a kid with a bowl cut. But those factors shouldn't have stopped me from setting my trajectory and controlling the factors I could have controlled to give me the best shot at my outcome. It's our job to load the spring in our favor so that it can push us toward our desired outcome.

But it can be easy to allow fear to creep in when we only consider the outcome goal:

- *What if your goal is to be with your ideal person and she rejects you?*

- *What if you aim all your anger and throw everything you have at the cancer diagnosis and your loved one dies anyway?*

- *What if you get excited about crushing your performance on stage and it completely flops?*

All of those outcomes are of course possible, but they are also largely outside of our control. All we can control is our trajectory, little by little, to the best of our ability. Because of the negativity bias of our brains (meaning that we feel negative events more intensely than positive ones, even if we experience both at the same arousal level), we are quick to consider only the potential costs of our actions that move toward our goals without considering the cost of inaction. We're unwilling to take the first small step forward, just in case it's a misstep.

But what if we are missing the bigger negative outcome by not taking action?

- *What if you don't approach that person but she was interested, too? Maybe you missed out on the love of your life!*

- *What if you could have beaten that diagnosis, but you never tried? How heavy will your regrets be?*

- *What if you get a standing ovation for your performance?*

Often, the passivity of not aiming, not trying, not taking that action, results in our deepest regrets. Psychologists Tom Gilovich and Shai Davidai found in their 2018 study that a whopping 76 percent of people regretted things that they could have done but did not.[58] Significantly more people regret not doing things than have regrets about the things they did try that didn't work out. The regrets we have when we take action reduce with time, while our regrets of inaction fester, and, according to at least one recent study, actually intensify with time.[59]

One of the reasons researchers believe this festering occurs is that, when we take action, we have the opportunity to learn and grow from the outcomes of that action. In contrast, inaction will always leave us wondering, **What if?**

I have very few regrets, but to be clear, I do have one big one. It's that I didn't figure out earlier that there was an implied second part to the oft-quoted Wayne Gretzky line, "You miss 100 percent of the shots you don't take."

Years after I retired from the sport, I look back at my basketball career and wonder how good I could have been if my coach had simply whispered to me, **"Hey, you're supposed to miss. That's part of the game."** In fact, even the professionals only average a shooting percentage of about 44 percent, which means the majority of the time, you're going to be taking shots you miss (especially as a young, developing player). That regret still festers, though.

What if I'd been willing to take action?

Setting Trajectories and Taking Action

When we springboard along a trajectory, we won't always get it right. We aren't guaranteed the outcomes we want (and almost certainly not right away!). Maybe you took that entrepreneurial leap, and it failed.

Great!

Now you have data to analyze.

TIME TO GET CURIOUS.

What went wrong? What do you need to do differently next time? How can you avoid the same mistakes in future opportunities?

But, the regrets of inactions don't give us any way to adjust our trajectory.

We sit on the edge of all that converted stress energy without ever putting it to action.

Inaction is the only way we feel like we can definitively control the outcome—even if it's a false sense of security. We must recognize that our job isn't to be certain: it's to be curious with that transformed stress energy, both in the moment and in reflecting upon the outcome. What is the smallest step forward you can take?

A trajectory is proximate. It's the action you take to move you immediately in the direction of your goal (or at least in the direction you believe will take you closer to your goal). The process of achieving your goal might take the form of multiple trajectories.

For example, let's say your finances are causing you stress. You invite the tiger in, fear (less), transfer that anxiety to excitement about how great it will feel to have some security, and set your goal to have $20,000 in your savings account by the end of the year. Several trajectories might get you there. Perhaps you decide to eat out a bit less, and cook for yourself more. (Bonus: you probably get healthier and maybe you even uncover a hidden joy of cooking!) Or maybe you recognize that you can pick up a side hustle with some of your spare time. Or perhaps it's as simple as contributing just a few more bucks from your paycheck to your savings account so that you have less to spend when you feel like having that weekend splurge.

EACH OF THESE TRAJECTORIES CELEBRATES SMALLER WINS ALONG THE WAY.

You could do all three, or just one, or alternate between them, but each action moves you in the direction of your goal. You can measure your progress, rather than feel discouraged when you open your bank account and see that you're still not there yet.

And the fun bit is that our brain actually rewards us for these small actions.

When we engage with our stress by setting and achieving a micro-goal, we trigger the activation of a circuit in our brain that releases the neurochemical dopamine, a molecule typically associated with reward.[60] It's also the molecule of motivation, drive, and addiction, so the more we move our stress along a trajectory that satisfies a micro-goal, the more we will repeat these behaviors in the future when we encounter another stressor (or the same stressor within the next day or hour!). It's a positive reinforcement loop that allows us to more effectively train our brains to work with us rather than against us as we channel our stress to achieve larger and heftier goals. Winning becomes neurologically addictive.

Small wins matter.

Most people get in trouble trying to point their trajectory toward huge outcome goals without setting process goals or steps along the way. Imagine that you set your trajectory on losing fifty pounds in the next six months. You might have a couple of days of weight loss, but by that second week, as you stop seeing changes, you quickly lose your motivation and start to fail. This reinforces stories in your head that your goals are never achievable and that you can't change, and you spiral back into that headspace where defeating thoughts win the day. Instead, when you work in small increments (for example, choosing a salad over pizza for lunch or taking an extra walk in the evening), you can reap the reward of dopamine hits for the little victories you have, reinforcing those behaviors and driving you toward bigger wins.

Your Turn:
STEERING
YOUR ENERGY

1. Identify Your Track
- What goal have you been avoiding?
- What conversation have you been putting off?
- What step have you been afraid to take?

2. Find Your First Turn
- What's the smallest possible way to start?
- What could you do today?
- How could you make the first try so small it's almost impossible to fail (and when you do it will still be worth it)?

3. Plan Your Recovery
- When (not if) you spin out, what's your immediate next step?
- Who can help you get back on track?
- What will you learn from each attempt?

One of my favorite stories about building these micro-trajectories comes from a friend of mine, Todd Duncan. As Todd tells it, he got in an Uber ride a few years ago, and the driver was morbidly obese. When he discovered that Todd was a motivational speaker, the driver said, "GREAT, motivate me! I've been trying to drop a hundred pounds for years, and I've never been successful." Todd got a bit more of the backstory. His driver ate four donuts to start the day. Rather than telling this man to start drinking green smoothies and eating celery, Todd nodded and said, "How about tomorrow you only eat three and a half donuts?" The trajectory was set, and the small win was to drop a tenth of a pound every day. It was the smallest possible increment that the driver's scale would measure. But, over the course of a year, that would mean dropping close to forty pounds! A feat he managed to accomplish and then some.

Small, incremental differences make massive changes and reinforce that you're on a trajectory that moves you forward. This is sometimes referred to as "The Winner's Effect."[61] Physical changes occur in your nervous and endocrine systems that encourage more of these positive behaviors (more to be excited about!). In fact, the more you win, the more winning affects you. Physiological changes in the brain after winning stimulate the production of more receptors for the hormones of winning, which means the effects of those hormones are increased, making the winner more sensitive to the win. Even at the molecular level, success breeds success.

For me, years after my festering regrets of not furthering my basketball career, my small-win trajectory meant getting back on the court. I called a friend who was a former player and coach and asked her to shoot around with me. After an hour or so of shooting, we played a little one-on-one. Sweaty, exhausted, and thoroughly happy, we agreed to meet again the following week. This continued for a few weeks before I had a wild idea. What if I went back to play college hoops? As far as I could tell, I still had four years of eligibility. I sheepishly introduced the idea to her. "How ridiculous would it be for me, a forty-two-year-old, to try out for a D1 team?" Her response will forever live in my happiest of memories. "Oh my goodness, why wouldn't you!? If I still had eligibility, I'd absolutely do it!" Together, we took one more small step forward.

She connected me to a player she had recruited who ran basketball programs, and I began playing with D1 athletes who had just graduated from UCLA and Iowa, as well as a few semi-pro players from overseas. I got back into lifting heavier weights. I made small wins every day toward my goal. Eventually, I got up the nerve to talk to the coach of the team I was hoping to play for. The fact that he burst out laughing when I told him what I was trying to accomplish shouldn't be held against him. After all, who in their right mind goes back to play basketball at an elite level when they've been out of the sport for over twenty years?! When he recovered from his shock, we had a great conversation, shook hands, and I felt one step closer. Which is why, when the call came from the NCAA compliance office that I wasn't eligible after all (apparently you have to compete within five years of beginning your undergraduate degree, and I was about twenty-five years too late), I was devastated.

What now?

Bounding Toward a Bigger Why—It's Not About You

Public speaking is a huge fear for most people. As a speaker, I often get asked how I can possibly do this for a living, day after day. Standing and speaking vulnerably in front of thousands of people is a recurring nightmare for most of us. For me, it's pure bliss. But that wasn't always the case. It took an incident early in my professional career to shift my thinking. At the time, I had been speaking just long enough to have gotten a little cocky, so when a parent overheard a piece of one of my speeches and asked if I would be willing to share a bit of my knowledge with some kids later that day, I was all in. The audience was to be an elite group of young male basketball players. I was hyped. Obviously, I knew the game and I had been a teacher after all, so I was totally prepared to handle teenage boys. **Or so I thought.**

Two minutes into my impromptu speech, I knew I had made a huge error.

They weren't getting it.

They were laughing and messing around.

I didn't have their attention, and I was beginning to look like a fool. My mind became a whirlwind of fear. These boys had transformed into tigers. Despite being more than twice their age, happily married, and a successful speaker, I felt like I was right back in high school, being judged and failing in front of the cool kids.

THAT'S WHEN I HAD MY EPIPHANY.
This wasn't about me.

It was about them—my audience. This shift in perspective was not just a mental trick; it was a profound change that aligned my goals with a bigger purpose.

In that moment, I began to see my role as a speaker—not as a performer who needed to earn the respect and love of her audience, but as a conduit for valuable information and inspiration. My goal was no longer to impress others, but to make a meaningful impact.

I realized:

1. **These kids are not tigers.**

2. **I had to embrace fear.** Instead of trying to calm down, I had to lean into the fear and run toward the roar. Convert the energy from stress into excitement.

3. **I had to direct my stress energy toward the actions I could control and aim my efforts at creating a positive impact for my audience.** I was stressed because I cared, but not about how I was being perceived. Rather, I cared whether or not I could make a difference. I couldn't win the battle of whether these kids would ultimately like or respect me (despite how desperately I had started out trying to prove myself to them), but I could show up now and give them my very best. I doubled down on what I believed these young minds needed to hear. I crafted my speech to address their

challenges, aspirations, and fears, and the energy in the room began to shift.

Ironically, I was teaching myself the same things I was teaching them as I spoke. You've done the work. You've shown up in practice and drilled. You have nothing to prove. You just have to go let your body do what you've trained it to do. Go all in and make an impact for your team. Forget about the rest. Forget about the score. Focus on the action you can take in a single play that will make a difference for the team. Don't worry about who you're playing against. Their game doesn't matter. You don't control how good they are. Your trajectory to perform at the highest level isn't threatened by how anyone else shows up.

They started to pay attention; the jokes and fidgeting ceased. Afterward, one of the students invited me to their game (an hour later). How could I resist? With eight seconds left on the clock, ahead by seven points to a team that by all measures should have pummeled them, the same kid found me in the crowd, locked eyes with me, and whispered, "Thank you." I still tear up thinking about that moment.

When we anchor our goals in something larger than individual gain or ego, we reduce the activity in the fear centers of our brain. What external impact do you have in achieving your goal? If you can focus on a bigger purpose, you reduce the psychological burden of personal performance and your attention naturally stays on task, rather than on self-evaluation. You can stay in the flow, rerouting your trajectory as often as needed, as you continually move toward your goal and a higher purpose.

IT WAS TIME FOR ME TO APPLY MY OWN LESSONS.

I couldn't play D1 ball. So what? That didn't mean I had to be done. My own mother, at seventy-two years old, was still playing on the Senior Olympics basketball team! Her generation had paved the way, brought us Title IX, and now women's basketball was taking off. What if, instead of focusing only on myself, I focused on something bigger—on an opportunity that would impact all of us women basketball players who weren't yet done playing? We shouldn't have to try to play at the D1 level just so we could get in a game or two in. I grabbed my friend, the basketball coach with whom I'd continued to play. At fifty-one, she was in the same boat as me. And there were others—older women players who just wanted a chance to *keep playing*. We scrambled to put together a website and platform for Gamechanger Basketball—a nonprofit to connect women basketball players across the country and help us all to keep playing. At the time of this writing, the community has just been launched. Maybe it will be a big flop. Maybe at the publication of this book, the community will have five thousand members! No matter the outcome, the trajectory forward and toward a larger purpose has driven me to a new level of stress (and joy!) that is much bigger than myself.

Discover Gamechanger Basketball here:

In the following section, we'll tackle stories of stress in the wild, but before you move on, think about the trajectory you want to point your stress energy along. What will it cost for you to *not* take action?

Stop playing sick.
YOUR FUTURE SELF IS BETTING ON YOU.

Curiosity and Fear Cannot Coexist

When setting your trajectory, here are a few questions I find most useful to begin with when moving toward a goal:

- *What story might help me succeed through the stress?*

- *What story am I telling myself that might not be true/accurate?*

- *How much will this matter in a month? A year? Five years?*

- *What might I learn from this?*

- *How will I grow from this experience?*

- *What is the smallest possible way to move forward?*

- *What good could come of this?*

- *What adventure might I have?*

- *What is the common enemy I want to use my anger to fight against?*

- *Why will this matter when I'm no longer part of this company/family/world?*

PART III

SPRINGBOARD IN ACTION

It can be tempting to think that once we achieve our goal, all the other puzzle pieces of our lives will magically fall into place. However, we often overlook the fact that life continues beyond that accomplishment. Without a new direction to pursue, this period can be quite unsettling.

Take, for example, the most decorated Olympian of all time, Michael Phelps. With twenty-eight Olympic medals, twenty-three of them gold, Phelps is widely regarded as one of the greatest athletes in the world. His achievements in swimming have resulted in numerous world records and redefined the standards of excellence in the sport. Yet despite his immense success, Phelps faced a deep emotional struggle after the 2012 London Olympics when he announced his plans to retire. In interviews, Phelps spoke openly about how, after achieving his ultimate goal—winning numerous gold medals—he felt a profound sense of emptiness and confusion about what to do next. Everything in his life had been focused on preparing for and winning at the Olympics, and once he had achieved what most people would consider the pinnacle of athletic success, he didn't know how to cope.

What comes next?

As much as we try to tie neat bows around chapters in our life like attaining a gold medal, marrying our sweetheart, or finally getting the promotion, there is no real discrete experience or event in life, save perhaps death.

OUR LIVES ARE ONE NEVER-ENDING, ALWAYS-EVOLVING STORY.

New tigers will find us, resurrecting and combining old fears with new struggles, opportunities, and change.

Welcome to real life.

The following section tackles stress in the wild—when we aren't just dealing with one discrete stressor at a time, and when life throws us tigers that knock us down for more than three minutes.

Chapter 7

The Compounding Stress SpringLoad

Objective:

Identify how compounding stress factors affect
your life and the lives of others around you,
and recognize that you aren't alone.

Defining the New PTSD:
Stress SpringLoad

I couldn't shut down. Even on my "vacation days" I felt on edge. When I was with my friends, I was constantly darting from conversation to conversation, afraid I was missing out on something. Then there were the pings on my phone. A family member. My husband. A work-related text. Had I responded to that, or did it get lost in the black hole of texts, DMs, and emails? At work, the twenty open tabs on my computer, three email inboxes, and meeting invites multiplying like rabbits made me feel like I'd never actually get any deep work done. At home, the dogs needed attention, dinner was never ready, laundry was piling up, and my time for sleep never felt like enough. It wasn't just a feeling—I wasn't making progress anywhere. At the end of every day, I felt like I was right back where I'd started, but with nothing to show for all my efforts. I was on a nonstop treadmill that certainly wasn't conditioning my health. Waking up at five was my only hope of actually moving the needle forward on work, but lately I'd found that even when I compromised my sleep for an early rise, I still wasn't being effective. My mind felt like a circus with monkeys running amok and elephants charging at me, while I, the ringmaster, was trying to stay calm while juggling fifty balls on the back of a spinning horse.

Dizzy. On edge. Irritable.

What had changed?

I used to be able to do this even after dancing until two in the morning and taking multiple shots of tequila. Was I just getting old, or had something broken in me?

EVERY DAY FELT LIKE I WAS MARCHING INTO BATTLE.

A micro-battle. I wasn't fighting battles like those where brave soldiers were risking their lives on the front lines every day, but my body was responding as if I were. And ultimately, it was this insight that would spark a massive shift in my life.

I began exploring the literature on Post-Traumatic Stress Disorder (PTSD), comparing my symptoms to those outlined by the National Institute of Mental Health:[62]

- *Negative thoughts about yourself, other people, or the world*
- *Hopelessness about the future*
- *Difficulty maintaining close relationships*
- *Feeling detached from family and friends*
- *Always being on guard for danger*
- *Self-destructive behavior, such as drinking too much or driving too fast*
- *Trouble sleeping*
- *Trouble concentrating*
- *Irritability, angry outbursts, or aggressive behavior*
- *Overwhelming guilt or shame*

My suspicion is that many of us can see a lot of these symptoms in ourselves. To be clear, I do *not* believe I was suffering from PTSD. But the more I recognized how often my body felt as if it were preparing for survival every day, the more I realized that these symptoms were indicative of something very real—not a single, time-compressed event of intense trauma (like we often see described in the PTSD literature), but a more subversive, subtle, continuous, compounding of daily stress: incremental microstressors stacking up on top of acute stressors, on top of chronic stressors. I thoroughly believe that most humans are facing a new kind of similar trauma—a Stress SpringLoad.

I was doing the work. I was breathing. Meditating. Self-caring. Admittedly, sometimes the self-care felt like added stress, like *have to* do this yoga class for my own health. But I was doing all the right things! I am a stress-physiologist for goodness' sake.

How is it that I can't pull my own shit together!?

But I'm not alone.

Our recent research study found that Americans are dealing with an average of about three types of major stressors every day (examples include financial concerns, relationship challenges, work pressures, news events, dealing with anxiety and depression, health concerns, moving, parenting challenges, drug or alcohol abuse, calendar overwhelm, and many more). You're not just handling one tiger at a time—you're actively juggling three of them while just trying to live your life! And under all this stress, more than half of Americans are likely to *reduce* self-care, with about six in ten people saying that they stress out even more while trying to reduce their stress!

NEARLY NINE IN TEN PEOPLE BELIEVED THAT STRESS WAS HAVING THE SAME CUMULATIVE EFFECT ON THEIR BODY AS TRAUMA.

In some sick way, I actually found these statistics comforting. "Okay, so I'm not the only loser who feels out of control with her stress!" But, from a much more pragmatic perspective, the findings of this research were devastating.

TRAUMA.

We are experiencing some form of collective, cumulative stress that feels like *trauma*.

After analyzing all of the data, I decided to take a bit of a risk in my work. As a professional speaker, trying new material is almost always a stressful event—it's not like you get to rehearse and see how well material goes over on practice audiences. To say that I was scared was an understatement. But, from my own work, I knew it wasn't a tiger. So I leaned in, literally at this point, to the microphone.

"If you knew me, you'd know I'm married to an Irish man, I have two dogs I adore, and I like to surf."

I paused, feeling my heart race and working through my own FEAR[less] Stress Formula steps.

This is my body preparing me for victory. My heart is delivering nutrients and oxygen to my brain to power me down this road I've wanted to explore for a while. This is going to help people.

I spoke again, a bit more slowly.

"If you really knew me, you'd know that I just got back from New York, where I managed at a distance to have a blow-up fight with my husband while in the middle of spending time with my father. There are multiple serious health scares happening in our immediate family right now, and I'm scared beyond words about what the next few years might bring."

You could hear the air vents purring after I spoke that sentence.

The thing I was finally willing to bet on was that I was not alone in my trauma-like experience of stress: We just don't talk about it. We talk about the stress of the upcoming deadline or trying to retain top talent. But we don't factor in all of the other compounding strains that we all bring with us to work. Whether or not we are consciously aware of the stressors, they are there—a Stress SpringLoad making us all feel disordered and like we're going to battle every day.

In subsequent talks, I would ask people to stand or raise their hands if *none* of the following stressors were currently affecting them or had affected them or a close loved one in the past year:

- *Illness/injury*
- *Retirement*
- *Moving*
- *Death*

- *Marriage or divorce*
- *Taking care of aging parents*
- *Newborn child*
- *Health issues*
- *Change in financial state*
- *Loss or change of job*
- *Cancer*
- *Incarceration*
- *Drug/alcohol abuse*
- *Family conflict*
- *Mental health (depression or anxiety)*

Of the thousands of people who had the opportunity to, not a single person raised their hand. Not one person stood.

Stress isn't going anywhere.

STRESS IS UBIQUITOUS AND SHARED.

And there is power in this recognition. Ironically, stress is something that can bring us together with formidable bonds if we let it. But that's a big "if." Consider the vulnerability of openly admitting your stressors—it can feel like yet another stressor, or the stress behind the stress, as it were.

When I attempted this material for the first time from stage, asking people to turn and introduce themselves to one another using the prompts, "If you knew me . . . " and then "If you really knew me . . . " I had a difficult time regaining control of the room. There was not a single person in the audience of five hundred who wasn't in tears. Something was happening here. The room was saturated with compassion, shared relief, and deep connection. I could almost taste the oxytocin.

Stress's secret superpower? It brings us together.

Most people are familiar with the hormone oxytocin as the "cuddle hormone," but it turns out that oxytocin is also one of the many hormones released in the early phases of the stress response.

As Dr. Kelly McGonigal, health psychologist and lecturer at Stanford University, beautifully illustrates in a 2021 interview with Dr. Heather Sandison:

> This is a stress response that biologically primes you to do two things—reach out to others for help and reach out to help others—and oxytocin increases your willingness to do both. It gives you the courage to ask for help, to ask for a hug, to let people know that you're struggling, but oxytocin also gives you courage to help others and it increases the warm glow that you get from being able to help others. . . . And as soon as you recognize, there are other people who are in it with you, there are people who've been through it before and have guidance to share. There are people who care about

you and want to help you through it. There are people who are in the same situation and worse off than you, and actually could use some of your insights and your strength. When you recognize any of those things, your brain is like, "Great. Let's not be alone for this because it's not a DIY stress." And then it increases levels of oxytocin specifically to ramp up those social instincts we have to reach out to others and it at the same time emboldens us. It gives us that courage and that hope that we need precisely when the stress is not a do-it-yourself challenge.[63]

I suspect this is where the "notable exception" applies from the employee well-being study mentioned in chapter 2 (see page 12–13). Of the ninety-plus stress management interventions explored in the study, only one demonstrated any significant improvement in well-being—doing charity or volunteer work. That fits perfectly within the FEAR[less] Stress Formula model. You're not trying to ignore or tamp down the tiger. Instead, you're transforming your stress energy into purposeful work, allowing the oxytocin to transform stressful times into an opportunity for community building.

Unfortunately, you can't just skip to the good part and get the oxytocin without also getting all of the other confounding stress hormones (cortisol, adrenaline, etc.). While these stress hormones have protective and positive effects in the short run, without proper management, they can be damaging in the long term.

THAT'S THE PARADOX OF STRESS.

We must ride the fear and anxiety up to that physiological state of arousal in order to have the energy to convert and point toward building community (or other noble causes). And while sometimes we might have the option to lean in on our own accord (for example, if we make a risky career move or raise our hand for that promotion that puts us in the hot seat), most of the time, stress isn't waiting for us to find it. It's hunting us. Taking that physiological ride up the side of the Yerkes-Dodson curve is usually less of a choice than we might wish for it to be.

Where in your life are you carrying significant amounts of stress? How can you shift your viewpoint of these stressors to see the potential they offer? More stress means more power. More energy. More opportunity to direct action toward meaning.

What are your top three stressors?

What's you first small step of action for each?

Remember This:

You're not failing at stress management. You're not alone. You're carrying a Stress SpringLoad that humans weren't designed to carry alone. But you don't have to do it alone.

In the next chapter, we'll explore how this Stress SpringLoad can turn into a powerful launchpad for growth.

Visualizing Your Stress SpringLoad

Think about your life at the moment. What are you carrying with you each day? Maybe you're worried about:

- *Your kid's performance at school*

- *Your exercise routine not being as stellar as it used to be*

- *The electric bill that is going to skyrocket this month with the cold snap*

- *That dinner party you're hosting on Friday*

- *Whether or not your partner will remember to book the dog sitter*

- *The ring of the phone that might be your mother needing your help*

- *That string of text messages you may have left unanswered, leaving your friend hanging*

- *Your friend's cancer diagnosis*

- *Oh yeah . . . and work! The tyranny of the inbox, your big presentation, where you're headed in the next five years . . .*

Or some variation on the above.

We are constantly carrying our present moments of stress to our daily routines, not to mention previous traumas like financial insecurity, emotional or physical abuse, or any other big-T or little-t traumas we carry forward in our behavioral patterns.

Try conceptualizing your own Stress SpringLoad here:

The cumulation of your Stress SpringLoad is measured using the following scientifically validated tools:

- **Early life experiences:** The ACES (Adverse Childhood Experiences) test is a tool used to assess the impact of childhood trauma on long-term health and well-being.[64] It was developed from a study conducted by the Centers for Disease Control and Prevention (CDC) and Kaiser Permanente in the late 1990s and involved over seventeen thousand participants.

- **Chronic long-term stressors:** The Chronic Stress Scale (CSS) is a tool designed to measure the persistent levels of stress experienced by an individual over an extended period.[65] The CSS focuses on long-term stressors and their impact on an individual's well-being.

- **Acute stressors:** The Perceived Stress Scale (PSS) is a psychological instrument designed to measure the perception of stress over the past month.[66] Developed by Sheldon Cohen and his colleagues in 1983, the PSS is one of the most widely used tools for assessing stress levels in research and clinical settings.

- **Microstressors:** The Mainz Inventory of Microstressors (MIMIS) is a psychological assessment tool designed to measure everyday, minor stressors, also known as microstressors—moments you might not even recognize at first as eliciting stress.[67] These microstressors can accumulate over time, especially in conjunction with other (acute/chronic/childhood-adversity) stressors, and impact our overall stress levels and well-being, despite each one being relatively minor on its own. The MIMIS was developed to fill a gap in stress-measurement tools by focusing specifically on these small, frequent stressors, rather than on major life events or chronic stress. The tool was created to provide a comprehensive and nuanced understanding of how minor daily hassles contribute to an individual's overall stress experience.

Each of these tests represents individually scientifically validated measures of stress that, when combined, offer the most comprehensive overview of your current stress state.

ACES Score: _____

Chronic Stress Score: _____

Acute Stress Score: _____

Microstress Score: _____

OVERALL STRESS SPRINGLOAD: _____

Chapter 8

Growing Through What We Go Through

Objective:
Recognize that often what we try to prevent in our lives is the very same thing that brings us meaning and purpose.

When I was eight years old, my house burned to the ground. It was just before Christmas, and my family had gathered with my aunts and uncles and cousins at our house to make gingerbread houses. We were happily gluing together gingerbread and singing Christmas carols when my father asked, "Does anybody else smell that?" We glanced around at one another for a moment before dismissing it as probably just some of the gingerbread burning. Thirty minutes later, my uncle perked up at the same thing my father had smelled earlier. Something was off, and the two of them disappeared to the back of the house out the sliding glass door to find a view that I can only imagine was horrific. The entire top half of the house was completely engulfed in flames. My father and uncle rushed back into the house, screaming for everyone to get out. Leaving everything behind, our family ran to safety across the street where our neighbors had already begun to gather. As a kid, I don't remember feeling any panic. Perhaps it was my curiosity that overrode the fear that might otherwise have overtaken me, but I remember watching with fascination, standing outside in the cold, upstate New York December weather, watching as the flames leaped into the night sky, making smoke and ash of our every possession. My parents were understandably concerned about the trauma this experience would mark upon my sister and me, but to this day, I count our house burning to the ground as one of the best things that ever happened to me.

THAT FIRE WAS SUCH A CLEAR TEACHER OF WHAT WAS AND WAS NOT IMPORTANT.

Stuff was just stuff.

My family was safe, and I'll never forget the way our community poured out love, support, and shelter. The very night of the fire, I had warm food in my belly, a roof over my head, and clothes for school the next day. A local farmer even sacrificed a lamb so we'd have something special for Christmas dinner.

It was truly a formative experience for me that, given the option, I'm certain my parents would have protected me from ever having to live through.

Our fear demands that we stay in control of outcomes, so we try our best to protect and shield ourselves and others.

But what if we are shielding ourselves from:

- *Positive changes in self-perception and interpersonal relationships?*
- *Greater self-awareness and self-confidence?*
- *A more open attitude toward others?*
- *A greater appreciation of life?*
- *The discovery of new possibilities?*

According to research conducted by Drs. Richard Tedeschi and Lawrence Calhoun, each of these aforementioned opportunities are available to us.[68] The caveat is that they come only after having gone through trauma.

In early January 2024, one of my best friends was diagnosed with stage 4 cancer out of the blue. She was a healthy, young, extremely fit individual who had been given a clean and clear health report just four months prior. To say that the news came as a shock is a massive understatement. Our friend group all felt the stress and anxiety that came with such a terrifying diagnosis— and I promise you it did not dissipate after those first three minutes of terror. None of us seemed to know exactly what to do. What can you do when you're given that news? We weren't given the choice. It's not a stressor I'd wish on my worst enemy, let alone my best friends, but there we were, riding that physiological wave up, with nothing we could do to change it, nothing we could do to "keep calm and carry on."

But what I witnessed over the next few months was one of the most profound experiences of my life. A pack formed. We had been a close-knit group of friends before this diagnosis, but this new stress truly transformed us. The tiger was clear and present. We'd acknowledged it, accepted its truth, and, in true stress-induced oxytocin form, began reaching out to one another. We cried. A lot. We laughed. We transferred the energy to anger . . . and productivity. We created a website to track treatments and meals and items that were needed for our sick friend and her wife. *We ran toward the roar.* We looked out for one another in a way that still chokes me up even now.

WE RAN TOWARD THE ROAR AND FOUND NEW MEANING OUTSIDE OF OURSELVES.

Even when a tiger insists there is nothing that can be done, even when we surely didn't want the tiger at the table, there it was, and along with it came a boatload of oxytocin. It was a chemical of courage, allowing us to bond more deeply and begin to transfer that fear and anxiety into something powerful and useful.

I can't end this story without sharing that three months after her terminal diagnosis, our friend, our warrior, walked out of her oncologist's office with a **perfectly clean scan.** Cue the tissues. She was the 1 percent who found a way through and kicked cancer's ass. She not only accepted the tiger, she raced with it, side by side, not trying to get rid of the stress or fear, but embracing it as a new part of her life. She leaned into hope with her wife, who had found a treatment only three weeks out from clinical trials. She leaned into our friend, an ER doctor, who helped make the calls to convince local oncologists to run the protocol. She leaned in to becoming the first person to ever receive this experimental treatment and took us all along for the ride with her. Today, as I write this, we are celebrating her six-month anniversary of a completely cancer-free scan.

Post-Traumatic Growth

While we've likely heard a lot about the highly researched Post-Traumatic Stress Disorder (PTSD), a condition that affects roughly 8 percent of Americans during their lifetimes, Post-Traumatic Growth (PTG) affects roughly 50 percent of people who endure trauma![69] Before developing their Post-Traumatic Growth Inventory, Tedeschi and Calhoun interviewed widows, prisoners of war, and people who had become dramatically disabled through horrific accidents.

In Jim Rendon's book *Upside*, the researchers quoted survivors as saying:[70]

- *"This was the one thing that happened in my life that I needed to have happened."*

- *"It was probably the best thing that ever happened to me."*

- *"If I hadn't experienced this and lived through it, I likely wouldn't be here today."*

- *"If I had to do it all over again, I would want it to happen the same way."*

These don't sound like statements you'd expect from people who had endured torture, abuse, paralysis, or other unimaginable experiences. I hear the echoes of people who have felt the tiger acutely, had outcomes outside of their control, and then used the residual energy of anger and excitement to redirect their trajectory toward a new positive direction.

To be clear, we're not hoping to encounter the trauma or pain or outcome we'd never wish on our own worst enemies. Our goal is simply to reposition those tigers.

Tedeschi says that,
"Post-Traumatic Growth is not happiness. It often coexists with distress."

It's where we focus that residual energy that makes all the difference.

For Michael Phelps, the trajectory shift came when he combined his passion for swimming with an advocacy for mental health, focusing outward on something bigger than his own accomplishments. Phelps began speaking openly about his struggles, which helped countless others open up and seek help for their own mental-health challenges. He founded the Michael Phelps Foundation, which is dedicated to teaching others to swim and providing a platform to overcome fears, boost self-esteem, and help educate and fight against the mental illnesses that one in five Americans struggle with. Michael Phelps had to move through the personal pain to find a purpose greater than himself.

Rhian Mannings, too, understands how stress and trauma can be cocreators of purpose in a profound way. Her story of Post-Traumatic Growth was reported in detail in a recent article from *The Guardian*.[71] In early 2012, Mannings was happily married to her beloved husband Paul, was a mother of three, and was celebrating her youngest son's one-year birthday. A week later, her one-year-old, George, was dead. One minute they had been playing and giggling together in the tub, and the next, George was having a seizure. Two hours later, a nurse brought the body of their youngest child to her and her husband. Only five days later, her rock, her husband, who blamed himself for the faultless death of their child, took his own life. Mannings describes the months that followed as an excruciating blur of torment.

Her turning point came not from suppressing her stress or memories, but from pointing that anger and hurt and pain into launching 2 Wish Upon A Star in 2014, her nonprofit that provides support to families trying to cope with sudden bereavement of a young person. In 2020, eight years after her devastating losses, Mannings was recognized with a Pride of Britain Award, and her nonprofit is working with police forces and emergency units in Wales to provide hundreds of people every year with the support that she and Paul never had.

None of us get to fully control the ride that life sets us on, but we ultimately do have a choice in what to do with our responses. We can linger in despair and wish for alternatives, or accept the cards we're dealt and move forward. That doesn't mean we won't ache for the past or for different outcomes. As Mannings so aptly stated, "I haven't moved on, but I have managed to move forward." And that statement fully encapsulates the Springboard stage. How do we find meaning in this emotion that moves us in a helpful direction?

Forward action in any direction allows us the gift of new data that we can analyze and then use to reassess and tweak our trajectory (or completely alter it).

I would assume that Mannings wasn't finding purpose or meaning in the initial aftermath and shock of losing her loved ones. When she first learned the news of her husband's passing just five days after the death of her son, she describes losing control of her bladder, vomiting, and being unable to care for herself for days. It would be strange in almost any acute traumatic event for anyone to immediately engage with the stress in a way that derives greater meaning and purpose from it.

BUT SETTING A TRAJECTORY IS NOT A ONE-OFF PROCESS—IT'S A CONTINUAL REAPPRAISAL OF EMOTIONS.

Remember the gift and curse of humans is our ability to revisit and re-elicit emotions after an event has passed. Hence the reason we grieve, ruminate, and yes, even laugh at memories. We have the ability, with curiosity, to continually return to our emotions, experience the tiger, and transfer the stress to an emotion that will set a new trajectory. For Mannings, it was anger in recognizing that services to help suddenly bereaved parents didn't exist when they lost George.

"Nobody told us that when a child dies, you're going to blame yourself, you're going to feel angry. We needed someone who understood to talk us through it, and that person never came. Someone should have been there to look after him and me," she says.

Believing Paul's death could have been prevented, Mannings became determined to change. Over time, that anxiety and distress she felt over losing her loved ones transformed into excitement that she could save others from feeling as isolated and alone as she did in her time of need.

While Mannings's cause is noble, and, with time, her trauma became easier to find deeper meaning in, I believe that far too many of us struggle to find our deeper purpose and meaning in our day-to-day stress. That's likely the result of us focusing too much on the individual nature of our goals rather than recognizing that as we change ourselves, we must also focus on changing the world around us.

We often take for granted all the systems in place that support us. Take, for example, the simple pleasure of a cup of coffee in the morning. From the farmers who grow the beans, to the suppliers of the water and agricultural equipment needed to support and harvest the fruits, to the manufacturers and operators of the roasters, to the educators and food safety teams supervising the quality of the product, to the packing and distributing teams, to the governing bodies that negotiated trade tariffs and FDA compliance, to the marketing and branding teams that designed the packaging, to the grocers who selected and stocked the product . . . the list is more extensive than I have room to detail.

The point is, we are far more integrally connected to communities than we often recognize or admit, and the more disconnected we become as we hyperfocus on our own stress, the more exacerbated that stress is likely to become—even when we're trying to resolve it.

This is one of the main points that social and psychological resilience researcher Dr. Michael Ungar argues in his description of Buddhist monks during an interview in which he describes rugged individualism as a major contributing factor of the stress epidemic:

> *The real story of Buddhist monks historically is not that they are simply beings seeking enlightenment. They live within cultures that feed them, house them, have the children who grow up to run the farms that grow the wheat and mill it and drag it up to the monastery to feed them. Their community conspires to allow this group of people to reach enlightenment, which is perceived as good for everybody around them. We so misunderstand that story as the individual seeking enlightenment. And that Buddhist nun down the street, the only reason she can do what she does is somehow resources . . . money . . . gets to her. But that is never the story we are told.*[72]

This is where I again want to return to the beginning of this book to the study exploring the failed outcomes of the ninety workplace wellness programs and interventions across over forty-six thousand individuals (see pages 12–13). The one notable exception to all of these failed self-help, individual-level focused interventions that actually improved well-being was community service. The data indicated significant improvement in participant well-being through an increased sense of purpose, accomplishment, social resources, and recovery.

THE FINAL KEY COMPONENT OF SETTING YOUR TRAJECTORY, THEN, IS POINTING IT OUTWARD FROM YOURSELF.

Rather than looking inward to self-care, how can you use this energy to care for others?

How does your goal benefit the community at large? While it may seem quite counterintuitive in a moment of stress and crisis to be looking for ways to care for other people, the recognition of "collective stress," or your community's stress, is a framework that very well might be the missing piece to your peace.

People who thrive are people who feel needed in some way, who feel integral to a community. Those who feel that they make beneficial contributions to their community are the same people who thrive through their stress because they can easily recognize their purpose in it. In the workplace, this is the classic story of employee engagement. Do I believe in the mission? Is my work connected to achieving that mission? Outside of work, the same principles apply to staying engaged in our lives.

When a devastating earthquake hit Haiti in 2010, many adults were killed, injured, and overwhelmed. Despite the trauma and loss, many children adapted quickly to lead the charge in rebuilding their hurting communities. Haitian culture places a strong emphasis on *konbit*, or collective effort and mutual support.[73] In Léogâne, one of the hardest-hit areas, a group of children formed a club called Les Petits Bâtisseurs (The Little Builders). They worked together to clean up debris, rebuild homes, and distribute lifesaving medicine and supplies to the elderly. The group advocated for their own rights, forming a community center where other children could safely play and receive informal education. A month after the earthquake, eleven-year-old Marie-Ange living in a nearby temporary settlement was asked, "What do you want most right now?" Her response? "I want to go to school." After clarifying that she was not in school prior to the earthquake, she was asked, "Why do you want to go now?"

"Because my country is broke, and I want to fix it."[74]

STRESS AND PURPOSE ARE TWO SIDES OF THE SAME COIN.

If these events all seem too large to fathom and you're wondering how you can find purpose in events less traumatic than earthquakes and horrific deaths of loved ones, let me offer one final story of my own trajectory through a significantly less dire stressful situation.

I'm not certain I had ever been more nervous in my life. To the right of me was the CEO of a multi-billion-dollar energy company.

To the left was a well-known and beloved television broadcaster who had interviewed all the big names in sports, entertainment, politics, and business. The room could hold a maximum of two hundred people, and the guests had an impressive array of degrees and accolades. At the center of the room stood the groom, Dr. Nick Morgan, looking striking and confident in his tuxedo.

While most people won't immediately recognize the name, you are most certainly familiar with his work. Nick has been brought in to critique the speeches of Barack Obama and the first official speech of Catherine, then–Duchess of Cambridge. A former fellow at the Center for Public Leadership at Harvard's Kennedy School of Government, Nick is a world-renowned speech coach, whose clients include A-listers from Yahoo executives, Emmy Award–winning talk show hosts, both of the previously described gentlemen on either side of me, and, somehow, me. I had been working with Nick for the past ten years, and while I certainly didn't know exactly how I fit in with this A-list of wedding attendees, I had grown close to Nick and was beyond honored when he asked if I would attend his wedding.

"OF COURSE!
I wouldn't miss it for the world!"

My response was genuine and unhesitating.

I love weddings.

I love Nick.

I love Boston.

Why was I sensing there was something more to this?

"I'd really like it if you'd be willing to say a few words," he continued. "I've curated a couple of other speakers I work with, and I think it would be fun to have you all do a short toast."

I swallowed hard.

A speech. To my world-renowned speech coach and his beloved bride. In front of his closest family and friends, on the most important day of his life. What could possibly go wrong? I could genuinely feel the bile rising even in that moment, months away from the actual wedding.

Which is how I found myself seated at the most intimidating table of my life. Sandwiched between legends who were looking equally as nervous. We were fumbling with our silverware, drinks untouched on the table as, one by one, we were called up to deliver our messages.

I had already invited the tiger in. I had said yes and was seated at the table moments before I was to be called up to deliver. Three minutes before go-time, I channeled my excitement, forcing a smile, keeping my chin up and shoulders back, repeating to myself, *You got this, you're excited, you're confident!* I felt my heart pounding and focused on the enhancing benefits this stress was providing my body. More blood. More oxygen. More focus to nail it.

Two minutes to go-time, I remind myself of the trajectories I'd set to get here.

You've practiced, you're ready—and then, switching to curiosity to stay out of fear . . .

Why would Nick invite you to do this if he didn't know you could nail it?

What is the best that can happen?

What do I want people to feel?

ONE MINUTE TO GO-TIME.

It wasn't about me.

This was about showing up for my community. For a person I loved. This mattered to me because this community mattered to me, and in that stress was meaning. Go-time. I stood and delivered not for me, not to prove myself, but to give a dear friend the message he deserved on that day.

Where can each of us point our trajectory, our stress, our energy and efforts toward something bigger than ourselves?

WHAT MORE WILL YOU DO FOR OTHERS, AS YOU FEAR LESS?

The stress isn't going away. But it just might be the catalyst for your greatest transformation. In our final chapter, we'll explore how to maintain hope when the stress feels overwhelming.

Chapter 9

Pointing Toward Hope

Objective:
Find peace in the fact that you're not to blame for shutting down in your stress and gather the hope it will take to push beyond it.

In the 1960s, psychologists Martin Seligman and Steven F. Maier conducted groundbreaking experiments that demonstrated how repeated exposure to uncontrollable stressors can lead to the belief that outcomes are beyond one's control.[75] Their most famous study resulted in a highly cited 1967 paper that still elicits strong emotional reactions today.

In this research, dogs were assigned to one of two experimental conditions. In each setup, the dogs were placed in a chamber where they received unsolicited and random electric shocks. For one group, these shocks were inescapable, and the dogs had no control over them (the "non-escape" group). For the other group (the "escape" group), the shocks could be turned off by pressing a panel with their nose (which these dogs quickly learned to do).

In the subsequent phase of the experiment, both groups of dogs were placed in a shuttle box—a divided space with a barrier. One side of the shuttle box was electrified, and the other was not. The barrier was low enough that the dogs could easily jump to the other side and escape the shocks. Remarkably, only the dogs from the "escape" group attempted to jump over the barrier. Having learned in the previous setup that escape was possible, these dogs wasted no time in finding a better environment. Tragically, the dogs assigned to the "non-escape" group made no attempt to leave the box. Even though safety was just on the other side of the easily jumpable barrier, they seemed resigned, accepting any shocks administered by the experimenters rather than making any effort to change the outcome.

These "non-escape" dogs had learned something profound:
HELPLESSNESS.

Their minds whispered, *Efforts are futile. We lack control.* Even when presented with an opportunity to escape, they remained passive, locked into a destiny they deemed manifest.

This learned helplessness occurs when repeated exposure to uncontrollable stressors leads to a belief that outcomes are beyond one's control, which can undermine one's motivation to change or alter the situation. It's as if hope itself retreats, leaving behind a void in which we exist, but don't really live. And this behavior certainly isn't limited to dogs.

Although extreme experiments like this are unethical for humans (and, many would argue, for dogs as well!), similar outcomes of learned helplessness have been initiated in humans with minor experimental manipulation.

In a series of studies, researchers introduced a loud, irritating noise to human subjects.[76] Participants were informed that solving a puzzle would turn off the noise. One group successfully learned that pressing buttons gave them control over their environment. However, a second group faced puzzles with no solutions, leaving them unable to silence the annoying noise.

To assess whether this learning would extend to other contexts, the same subjects, along with new participants, encountered similar situations but with novel problem types.

The problems in this phase were identical, ensuring both groups had an equal chance of solving them. Those who could previously turn off the annoying sound performed as well as new subjects. In contrast, those who experienced the unsolvable condition earlier performed significantly worse. Similar to the dogs in the original experiments, the human subjects inaccurately generalized their learned helplessness to a new situation, believing that their circumstances were beyond their control.

I'm sure there are many of us that feel like we're in this experiment right now.

How many times do we clear our inbox only to return from our triumphant coffee break to be buried in messages again?

What other "shocks" are you readily accepting as "just how it is"? What barrier are you not jumping over because you think it will be just as bad on the other side?

What alarms are you ignoring because you think you have no control over the blaring sounds of daily life?

I think this is where many of us have arrived in our journey with stress: *learned helplessness*.

We've tried yoga and meditation and all the self-care books we can stand, and yet, here we are, still being shocked by the anxiety and overwhelm of daily existence.

Seligman, one of the original researchers of learned helplessness, would later propose an antidote:

LEARNED HOPEFULNESS.

Just as despair can be learned, so, too, can new formulas for reclaiming agency.

And that is the message at the core of this book: reclaiming agency from the hauntings of anxiety and fear that leave us shaking in the confines of our metaphorical cages. We are more powerful than we recognize in reshaping our stress responses to work for us.

Fifty years after Seligman and Maier initially coined the term learned helplessness, they revisited their work and made some surprising discoveries.[77] This passivity to electric shocks or other unpreferred circumstances is not *learned*. It's the default response of a neural network turned on by prolonged aversive events. You aren't sitting there accepting the shocks—being complicit in your stress and overwhelm—because you've learned to. Your brain is wired to shut down your own escape from suffering.

Now the good news.

You can overcome this passive response by learning that you have control.

YOU DON'T HAVE TO STAY STUCK.

We can overcome helplessness by looking forward to the future.

The key question seems to be:

What (even small thing) can I control in these adverse circumstances?

THE ANSWER IS INVITING THE TIGERS IN, TRANSFERRING OUR ENERGY, AND SETTING SMALL TRAJECTORIES FORWARD.

We don't get to control the stress, or our arousal state, but we certainly do have control over its interpretation and how we utilize it to move us in a different direction.

We don't have to unlearn helplessness; we only need to learn to take action for a better future.

This is what sparks hope.

BUILDING HOPE PROTOCOL

1. List Your Stress Points & Recognize Reality

- What feels overwhelming?
- Where do you feel stuck?
- What seems hopeless?

2. Find Your Control Points. For Each Stressor, Identify:

- What you can't control (accept this)
- What you can influence (focus here)
- One tiny step forward (take this action today)

3. Build Your Support System

- Who can help? Who will this help?
- What resources exist? What more will you need?
- Where can you find or build community?

HOPE IS NOT MERE WISHFUL THINKING.

When we express sentiments like, "I hope I pass my exam," or "I hope I get the promotion," we're creating a mindset that implies that external factors alone determine these outcomes. But hope stands apart as a powerful positive emotion, reminding us of our capacity to exert influence over and progress toward our objectives, specifically because we feel it amid adversity and obstacles. We have the power, in all the chaos and stress that life brings, to lean in and find a way to move forward.

In the heart of the Vietnam War, Admiral James Stockdale found himself imprisoned in the infamous Hoa Lo Prison, ironically nicknamed by some of its prisoners as "Hanoi Hilton" for its flagrant contrast with the luxuries of the American hotel.[78]

Conditions in the prison were notoriously brutal—endless days of torture, isolation, and uncertainty. Yet, Stockdale famously emerged as a beacon of resilience and wisdom. He didn't cling to false hopes or set arbitrary deadlines for his release. Instead, he confronted the stark reality of his situation.

He invited the tiger in.

He knew he was in for the long haul, facing unimaginable suffering, and so he used that stress in novel ways. He transferred that stress energy to anger, beating himself with a wooden stool so he couldn't be paraded in front of the press as an example of the good conditions in the prison. He transferred that stress energy to excitement and set trajectories toward connection and a purpose larger than himself by developing an elaborate communications system that included tap codes and the swish-swashing of a mop to communicate important messages to his men.

Stockdale believed he would prevail, that this harrowing experience would shape him profoundly. His mindset wasn't blind positivity; it was a resilient balance between acknowledging the tiger and controlling what he could within those circumstances in order to provide hope.

Finding our own springboard for stress, just like finding hope, isn't wishful thinking alone—it's a skill that we practice and earn.

Like hope, our opportunity to springboard with stress is sparked by negativity and uncertainty.

WE MUST INVITE THE TIGER IN.

It is a unique paradox, that we require stress and challenges to become all we are meant to be.

You have the tools, the mindset, and likely, also the stress to make your own shift remarkable.

It's time to put these tools to work, to recognize that more stress only means more power, more energy, more opportunity:

To fear less,

and become

so much more.

Here's to the little leaps and the springboards that can shoot you soaring toward new heights . . .

if you are willing to dare.

Notes

1   Pizzino, Gabriele, Natasha Irrera, Mariapaola Cucinotta, et al. "Oxidative Stress: Harms and Benefits for Human Health." *Oxidative Medicine and Cellular Longevity* (2017). https://doi.org/10.1155/2017/8416763.

2   Khoury, Reine and Corina Nagy. "Running from Stress: A Perspective on the Potential Benefits of Exercise-Induced Small Extracellular Vesicles for Individuals with Major Depressive Disorder." *Frontiers in Molecular Biosciences 10* (2023). https://doi.org/10.3389/fmolb.2023.1154872.

3   American Psychological Association. "Studies Show Normal Children Today Report More Anxiety Than Child Psychiatric Patients in the 1950s." December 14, 2000. https://www.apa.org/news/press/releases/2000/12/anxiety.

4   World Health Organization. "COVID-19 Pandemic Triggers 25% Increase in Prevalence of Anxiety and Depression Worldwide." March 2, 2022. https://www.who.int/news/item/02-03-2022-covid-19-pandemic-triggers-25-increase-in-prevalence-of-anxiety-and-depression-worldwide.

5   Rose, Macala. "What Self-Care Trends Means for Retailers in 2024." ASK Market Week. May 8, 2024. https://asdonline.com/blog/retail-news/what-self-care-trends-mean-for-retailers-in-2020/#:~:text=Four%20years%20ago%2C%20we%20began,into%20the%20self%2Dcare%20trend.

6   Global Wellness Institute. *Health, Happiness, and the Wellness Economy: An Empirical Analysis.* Global Wellness Institute, 2023.

7   Tlalka, Stephany. "Meditation Is the Fastest Growing Health Trend in America." Mindful. December 11, 2018. https://www.mindful.org/meditation-is-the-fastest-growing-health-trend-in-america/.

8   Wei, Marlynn. "New Survey Reveals the Rapid Rise of Yoga—And Why Some People Still Haven't Tried It." Harvard Health Publishing. March 7, 2016. https://www.health.harvard.edu/blog/new-survey-reveals-the-rapid-rise-of-yoga-and-why-some-people-still-havent-tried-it-201603079179.

[9] Fleming, William J. "Employee Well-Being Outcomes from Individual-Level Mental Health Interventions: Cross-Sectional Evidence from the United Kingdom." *Industrial Relations Journal* 55, no. 2 (2024): 162–182. https://doi.org/10.1111/irj.12418.

[10] Barry, Ellen. "Workplace Wellness Programs Have Little Benefit, Study Finds." *New York Times.* January 15, 2024. https://www.nytimes.com/2024/01/15/health/employee-wellness-benefits.html.

[11] Bethune, Brian. "When It Comes to Resilience, the Self-Help Industry Has It All Wrong." Maclean's. May 23, 2019. https://macleans.ca/society/when-it-comes-to-resilience-the-self-help-industry-has-it-all-wrong/.

[12] Yerkes, Robert M. and John D. Dodson. "The Relation of Strength of Stimulus to Rapidity of Habit-Formation." *Journal of Comparative Neurology and Psychology* 18, no. 5 (1908): 459–482. https://doi.org/10.1002/cne.920180503.

[13] Corbett, Martin. "From Law to Folklore: Work Stress and the Yerkes-Dodson Law." *Journal of Managerial Psychology* 30, no. 6 (2015): 741–752. https://doi.org/10.1108/JMP-03-2013-0085.

[14] Khoury, Bassam, Tania Lecomte, Guillaume Fortin, et al. "Mindfulness-Based Therapy: A Comprehensive Meta-Analysis." *Clinical Psychology Review* 33, no. 6 (2013): 763–771. https://doi.org/10.1016/j.cpr.2013.05.005.

[15] Crum, Alia J., Peter Salovey, and Shawn Achor. "Rethinking Stress: The Role of Mindsets in Determining the Stress Response." *Journal of Personality and Social Psychology* 104, no. 4 (2013): 716–733. https://psycnet.apa.org/doi/10.1037/a0031201.

[16] Ezzati, Ali, Julie Jiang, Mindy J. Katz, Martin J. Sliwinski, Molly E. Zimmerman, and Richard B. Lipton. "Validation of the Perceived Stress Scale in a Community Sample of Older Adults." *International Journal of Geriatric Psychiatry* 29, no. 6 (2014): 645–652. https://doi.org/10.1002/gps.4049.

[17] Peabody, Jeremy E., Rebecca Ryznar, Markus T. Ziesmann, and Lawrence Gillman. "A Systematic Review of Heart Rate Variability as a Measure of Stress in Medical Professionals." *Cureus* 15, no. 1 (2023). https://doi.org/10.7759/cureus.34345.

18   Heiss, Rebecca. Pre-T-3 Trial Stress Assessment. Cognito Forms. Accessed November 15, 2024. https://www.cognitoforms.com/RebeccaHeiss/PreT3TrialStressAssessment.

19   Sapolsky, Robert M. "How to Relieve Stress." *Greater Good Magazine*. March 22, 2012. https://greatergood.berkeley.edu/article/item/how_to_relieve_stress.

20   Lewis, Carroll. *Alice's Adventures in Wonderland*. Broadview Press, 2000.

21   Luo, Michael. "Excuse Me. May I Have Your Seat?" *New York Times*. September 14, 2004. https://www.nytimes.com/2004/09/14/nyregion/excuse-me-may-i-have-your-seat.html.

22   Eisenberger, Naomi I., Matthew D. Lieberman, Kipling D. Williams. "Does Rejection Hurt? An FMRI Study of Social Exclusion." *Science* 302, no. 5643 (2003): 290–292. https://doi.org/10.1126/science.1089134.

23   Woolley, Kaitlin and Ayelet Fishbach. "Motivating Personal Growth by Seeking Discomfort." *Psychological Science* 33, no. 4 (2022): 510–523. https://doi.org/10.1177/09567976211044685.

24   Seinfeld Clips. "Seinfeld Elaine's Dance." YouTube video, 00:29. August 9, 2022. https://www.youtube.com/watch?v=_NxIo6a6sHk.

25   Gaziano, Thomas, K. Srinath Reddy, Fred Paccaud, Sue Horton, and Vivek Chaturvedi. "Chapter 33: Cardiovascular Disease." In *Disease Control Priorities in Developing Countries*. 2nd edition. Oxford University Press, 2006. https://www.ncbi.nlm.nih.gov/books/NBK11767/#:~:text=Cardiovascular%20disease%20(CVD)%20is%20the,Lopez%201996%3B%20WHO%202002b).

26   Orth, Taylor. "Three in 10 Americans Fear Snakes—And Most Who Do Fear Them a Great Deal." YouGov. June 26, 2022. https://today.yougov.com/society/articles/42863-americans-fear-snakes-heights-spiders-poll.

27   Chippaux, Jean-Philippe. "Incidence and Mortality Due to Snakebite in the Americas." *PLOS Neglected Tropical Diseases* 11, no. 6 (2017). https://doi.org/10.1371/journal.pntd.0005662.

28   CDC. "Heart Disease Facts." October 24, 2024. https://www.cdc.gov/heart-disease/data-research/facts-stats/index.html#:~:text=Heart%20disease%20is%20the%20leading,lost%20productivity%20due%20to%20death.

29   McGehee, Lucy. "Cause of Death: Vending Machine." American University Core. Accessed November 15, 2024. https://edspace.american.edu/atrium/portfolio-item/mcgehee-lucy-cause-of-death/#:~:text=According%20to%20the%20United%20States,irrational%20side%20to%20human%20behavior.

30   Bansal, Agam, Chandan Garg, Abhijith Pakhare, and Samiksha Gupta. "Selfies: A Boon or Bane?" *Journal of Family Medicine and Primary Care* 7, no. 4 (2018): 828–831. https://doi.org/10.4103/jfmpc.jfmpc_109_18.

31   Hannan, Scott E. and David F. Tolin. "Mindfulness and Acceptance-Based Behavior Therapy for Obsessive-Compulsive Disorder." *Acceptance and Mindfulness-Based Approaches to Anxiety* (2016): 271–299. https://doi.org/10.1007/0-387-25989-9_11.

32   LeWine, Howard E. "Understanding the Stress Response." Harvard Health Publishing. April 3, 2024. https://www.health.harvard.edu/staying-healthy/understanding-the-stress-response.

33   Baumeister, Roy F., Kathleen D. Vohs, Jennifer L. Aaker, and Emily N. Garbinsky. "Some Key Differences Between a Happy Life and a Meaningful Life." *The Journal of Positive Psychology* 8, no. 6 (2013): 505–516. http://dx.doi.org/10.1080/17439760.2013.830764.

34   Young, Jeremy C. "Was Teddy Roosevelt a Good Public Speaker?" Fifteen Eighty Four (blog). Cambridge University Press. August 10, 2017. https://cambridgeblog.org/2017/08/was-teddy-roosevelt-a-good-public-speaker/.

35   Theodore Roosevelt Center. "The Man in the Arena." Accessed November 15, 2024. https://www.theodorerooseveltcenter.org/Learn-About-TR/TR-Encyclopedia/Culture-and-Society/Man-in-the-Arena.aspx.

36   American Adoptions. "How Many Couples Are Waiting to Adopt a Baby?" Accessed November 15, 2024. https://www.americanadoptions.com/pregnant/waiting_adoptive_families#:~:text=While%20it%20is%20difficult%20to,who%20is%20placed%20for%20adoption.

[37]   Petrolini, Valentina and Marco Viola. "Core Affect Dynamics: Arousal as a Modulator of Valence." *Review of Philosophy and Psychology* 11 (2020): 783–801. https://doi.org/10.1007/s13164-020-00474-w.

[38]   Nielen, M.M.A., D.J. Heslenfeld, K. Heinen, et al. "Distinct Brain Systems Underlie the Processing of Valence and Arousal of Affective Pictures." *Brain and Cognition* 71, no. 3 (2009): 387–396. https://doi.org/10.1016/j.bandc.2009.05.007.

[39]   Wood Brooks, Alison. "Get Excited: Reappraising Pre-Performance Anxiety as Excitement." *Journal of Experimental Psychology: General* 143, no. 3 (2013): 1144–1158. https://doi.org/10.1037/a0035325.

[40]   Keller, Abiola, Kristin Litzelman, Lauren E. Wisk, et al. "Does the Perception That Stress Affects Health Matter? The Association with Health and Mortality." *Health Psychology* 31, no. 5 (2012): 677–684. https://doi.org/10.1037/a0026743.

[41]   The American Cancer Society medical and editorial content team. "Key Statistics for Melanoma Skin Cancer." Last modified January 17, 2024. https://www.cancer.org/cancer/types/melanoma-skin-cancer/about/key-statistics.html#:~:text=About%20100%2C640%20new%20melanomas%20will,5%2C430%20men%20and%202%2C860%20women).

[42]   Jamieson, Jeremy P., Matthew K. Nock, and Wendy Berry Mendes. "Mind over Matter: Reappraising Arousal Improves Cardiovascular and Cognitive Responses to Stress." *Journal of Experimental Psychology: General* 141, no. 3 (2011): 417–422. https://doi.org/10.1037/a0025719.

[43]   Stilwell, Blake. "The True Origin of the US Marine Corps' 'Oorah' Call." Military.com. February 6, 2023. https://www.military.com/history/true-origin-of-us-marine-corps-oorah-call.html.

[44]   Beck, Cam. "The Origin of OO-RAH." OO-RAH.com. Accessed November 15, 2024. https://www.oo-rah.com/perspectives/the-origin-of-oo-rah.

[45]   Jordan, Kevin D. and Akiko Okifuji. "Anxiety Disorders: Differential Diagnosis and Their Relationship to Chronic Pain." *Journal of Pain & Palliative Care Pharmacotherapy* 25, no. 3 (2011): 231–245. https://doi.org/10.3109/15360288.2011.596922.

[46]   Mazzone, Luigi, Francesca Ducci, Maria Cristina Scoto, Eleonora Passaniti, Valentina Genitori D'Arrigo, and Benedetto Vitiello. "The Role of Anxiety Symptoms in School Performance in a Community Sample of Children and Adolescents." *BMC Public Health* 7, no. 347 (2007). https://doi.org/10.1186/1471-2458-7-347.

[47]   Raghunathan, Rajagopal, Michael T. Pham, and Kim P. Corfman. "Informational Properties of Anxiety and Sadness, and Displaced Coping." *Journal of Consumer Research* 32, no. 4 (2006): 596–601. https://doi.org/10.1086/500491.

[48]   Eysenck, Michael W. and Manuel G. Calvo. "Anxiety and Performance: The Processing Efficiency Theory." *Cognition and Emotion* 6, no. 6 (1992): 409–434. https://doi.org/10.1080/02699939208409696.

[49]   Bandura, Albert. *Self-Efficacy: The Exercise of Control.* W. H. Freeman, 1997.

[50]   Wood Brooks, Alison. "Get Excited: Reappraising Pre-Performance Anxiety as Excitement." *Journal of Experimental Psychology: General* 143, no. 3 (2013): 1144–1158. https://doi.org/10.1037/a0035325.

[51]   Woodruff, C. Chad. "Reflections of Others and of Self: The Mirror Neuron System's Relationship to Empathy." *The Neuroscience of Empathy, Compassion, and Self-Compassion* (2018): 157–187. https://doi.org/10.1016/B978-0-12-809837-0.00006-4.

[52]   Davis, J.I., A. Senghas, F. Brandt, and K.N. Ochsner. "The Effects of BOTOX Injections on Emotional Experience." *Emotion* 10, no. 3 (2010): 433–440. https://psycnet.apa.org/doi/10.1037/a0018690.

[53]   Strack, F., L.L. Martin, and S. Stepper. "Inhibiting and Facilitating Conditions of the Human Smile: A Nonobtrusive Test of the Facial Feedback Hypothesis." *Journal of Personality and Social Psychology* 54, no. 5 (1988): 768–777. https://doi.org/10.1037//0022-3514.54.5.768.

[54]   Cuddy, Amy. "Your Body Language May Shape Who You Are." TED Talk Video, 20:45. June 2012. https://www.ted.com/talks/amy_cuddy_your_body_language_may_shape_who_you_are?subtitle=en.

[55]   Elkjaer, Emma, Mai B. Mikkelsen, Johannes Michalak, Douglas S. Mennin, and Mia S. O'Toole. "Expansive and Contractive Postures and Movement: A Systematic Review and Meta-Analysis of the Effect of Motor Displays on Affective and Behavioral Responses." *Association for Psychology Science* 17, no. 1 (2020). https://doi.org/10.1177/1745691620919358.

[56]   Lench, H.C., N.T. Reed, T. George, K.A. Kaiser, and S.G. North. "Anger Has Benefits for Attaining Goals." *Journal of Personality and Social Psychology* 126, no. 4 (2024): 587–602. https://psycnet.apa.org/doi/10.1037/pspa0000350.

[57]   Baas, Matthijs, Carsten K.W. De Dreu, and Bernard A. Nijstad. "Creative Production by Angry People Peaks Early On, Decreases over Time, and Is Relatively Unstructured." *Journal of Experimental Social Psychology* 47, no. 6 (2011): 1107–1115. https://doi.org/10.1016/j.jesp.2011.05.009.

[58]   Davidai, S. and T. Gilovich. "The Ideal Road Not Taken: The Self-Discrepancies Involved in People's Most Enduring Regrets." *Emotion* 18, no. 3 (2018): 439–452. https://psycnet.apa.org/doi/10.1037/emo0000326.

[59]   Gilovich, T. and V.H. Medvec. "The Experience of Regret: What, When, and Why." *Psychological Review* 102, no, 2 (1995): 379–395. https://psycnet.apa.org/doi/10.1037/0033-295X.102.2.379.

[60]   Baik, Ja-Hyun. "Stress and the Dopaminergic Reward System." *Experimental & Molecular Medicine* 52 (2020): 1879–1890. https://doi.org/10.1038/s12276-020-00532-4.

[61]   Fuxjager, Matthew J. and Catherine A. Marler. "How and Why the Winner Effect Forms: Influences of Contest Environment and Species Differences." *Behavioral Ecology* 21, no. 1 (2010): 37–45. https://doi.org/10.1093/beheco/arp148.

[62]   National Institute of Mental Health. "Post-Traumatic Stress Disorder." Last modified May 2024. https://www.nimh.nih.gov/health/topics/post-traumatic-stress-disorder-ptsd.

[63]   Sandison, Heather. "How Stress Can Make You Resilient: An Interview with Kelly McGonigal, Ph.D." Qualia. April 29, 2021. https://www.qualialife.com/how-stress-can-make-you-resilient-an-interview-with-kelly-mc-gonigal-ph-d.

[64]   Murphy, Anne, Howard Steele, Miriam Steele, Brooke Allman, Theodore Kastner, and Shanta Rishi Dube. "The Clinical Adverse Childhood Experiences (ACEs) Questionnaire: Implications for Trauma-Informed Behavioral Healthcare." *Integrated Early Childhood Behavioral Health in Primary Care* (2016): 7–16. https://doi.org/10.1007/978-3-319-31815-8_2.

[65]   Wheaton, B. Chronic Stress Measure [Database record]. APA PsycTests, 1991. https://doi.org/10.1037/t11307-000.

[66]   Ezzati, Ali, Julie Jiang, Mindy J. Katz, Martin J. Sliwinski, Molly E. Zimmerman, and Richard B. Lipton. "Validation of the Perceived Stress Scale in a Community Sample of Older Adults." *International Journal of Geriatric Psychiatry* 29, no. 6 (2013): 645–652. https://doi.org/10.1002/gps.4049.

[67]   Chmitorz, Andrea, Karolina Kurth, Lara K. Mey, et al. "Assessment of Microstressors in Adults: Questionnaire Development and Ecological Validation of the Mainz Inventory of Microstressors." *JMIR Mental Health* 7, no. 2 (2020). https://doi.org/10.2196/14566.

[68]   Tedeschi, Richard G. and Lawrence G. Calhoun. "Target Article: 'Posttraumatic Growth: Conceptual Foundations and Empirical Evidence.'" *Psychological Inquiry* 15, no. 1 (2004): 1–18. https://doi.org/10.1207/s15327965pli1501_01.

[69]   National Institute of Mental Health. "Post-Traumatic Stress Disorder (PTSD)." Accessed November 18, 2024. https://www.nimh.nih.gov/health/statistics/post-traumatic-stress-disorder-ptsd.

[70]   Rendon, Jim. *Upside: The New Science of Post-Traumatic Growth.* Touchstone, 2015.

[71]   Sarner, Moya. "Post-Traumatic Growth: The Woman Who Learned to Live a Profoundly Good Life After Loss." *The Guardian.* May 11, 2021. https://www.theguardian.com/lifeandstyle/2021/may/11/post-traumatic-growth-the-woman-who-learned-to-live-a-profoundly-good-life-after-loss.

[72]   Bethune, Brian. "When It Comes to Resilience, the Self-Help Industry Has It All Wrong." Maclean's. May 23, 2019. https://macleans.ca/society/when-it-comes-to-resilience-the-self-help-industry-has-it-all-wrong/.

[73] Michel, Jéruscha Vasti. "Taking the Lead: Youth in Haiti Take Action in Response to the Recent Earthquake." United Nations Haiti. September 22, 2021. https://haiti.un.org/en/145517-taking-lead-youth-haiti-take-action-response-recent-earthquake.

[74] Better Care Network. *UNICEF Situation Update: Children in Haiti One Month After.* 2010. https://bettercarenetwork.org/sites/default/files/Unicef%20Situation%20Update%20-%20Children%20in%20Haiti%20One%20Month%20After.pdf.

[75] Seligman, Martin E. and Steven F. Maier. "Failure to Escape Traumatic Shock." *Journal of Experimental Psychology* 74, no. 1 (1967): 1–9. https://psycnet.apa.org/doi/10.1037/h0024514.

[76] Hiroto, Donald S. and Martin E. Seligman. "Generality of Learned Helplessness in Man." *Journal of Personality and Social Psychology* 31, no. 2 (1975): 311–327. https://psycnet.apa.org/doi/10.1037/h0076270.

[77] Maier, Steven F. and Martin E.P. Seligman. "Learned Helplessness at Fifty: Insights from Neuroscience." *Psychological Review* 123, no. 4 (2016): 349–367. https://doi.org/10.1037/rev0000033.

[78] Congressional Medal of Honor Society. "James Bond Stockdale." Accessed November 18, 2024. https://www.cmohs.org/recipients/james-b-stockdale.

Acknowledgments

This book would not have been possible without the contributions, support, and love of so many people.

First, to my family—for all the stress I caused you, I hope the ideas in this book give you some peace. UD, this one is especially for you. For your bravery and the unwavering JOY you bring to the world. You are an unceasing inspiration to me and so many others. Keep running at the roar.

To my second family—Leigh, Keri, Liz, Mel, Charlotte, Bethany, (Elliott and Trevor), Haley, Erin, Cole, BJ, Danielle, Shane, Casey, and all of my Gamechanger women—Each of you has been a springboard for me to launch from. I'm so grateful to be surrounded by such empowered and empowering humans.

To my speaking friends and colleagues—thank you for being my greatest audiences and pushing me every day to be better.

To my Achara team—thank you for helping me continuously seek joy in work and relationships.

To the Ideapress team—for your patience, guidance, and for believing in my work.

To Kendra—my absolute badass designer, for your creativity and insights I'll forever be indebted.

To my husband, **Dermot Jevens**—for your editorial help (even when I resisted). But far more importantly, for your love and support. I am able to run as hard and fast as I do because you always provide me with a safe place to land.

To my **readers and audiences**—thank you for taking the time to engage with me and this book. Your curiosity and enthusiasm inspire me daily.

Finally, **to everyone who shared their knowledge, stories, and stress with me along the way**—thank you for giving my life meaning. May we all continue to live very stressful, purposeful lives.

About the Author

Dr. Rebecca Heiss hails from a small town in upstate New York—shout-out to Norwich! She grew up playing basketball and football in the backyard with her sister and neighborhood kids. Basketball stuck with her, and she continues to enjoy playing with friends today while promoting her cofounded nonprofit, Gamechanger.

Aside from sports, Rebecca's passion is helping others find their fear(less). As an academic with a love of teaching, she finds nothing more rewarding than watching a light bulb go on for people when they finally stop fighting against their stress. Whether you're a CEO of a Fortune 500 company, a parent, or an athlete (or all three!), Rebecca believes your best performance, deepest purpose, and greatest joy all lie just on the other side of fear.

Rebecca is a full-time keynote speaker residing in Greenville, South Carolina, with her spoiled rotten dogs, Guinness and Murphy (and her beloved husband). If you bump into her out running the trail, ask her about biting lemons, her failed app, walking 500 miles across Spain, her perfect ice cream recipe, or crows (and settle in for some stories!).

Index